# BRANCHES
# &
# BLOOMS

# BRANCHES
# &
# BLOOMS

A Step-by-Step Guide to Creating Magical Centerpieces, Wreaths,
Garlands, and Other Unexpected Arrangements

*Alethea Harampolis and Jill Rizzo of Studio Choo*
*Photographs by Paige Green*

ARTISAN
NEW YORK

Library of Congress Cataloging-in-Publication Data

Names: Harampolis, Alethea, author. | Rizzo, Jill, author.
Title: Branches & blooms / Alethea Harampolis and Jill Rizzo
    of Studio Choo.
Other titles: Wreath recipe book | Branches and blooms
Description: New York : Artisan, 2017. | "Originally published
    as The Wreath Recipe Book."
Identifiers: LCCN 2016032077 | ISBN 9781579657611 (pbk.)
Subjects: LCSH: Wreaths.
Classification: LCC TT899.75 .H37 2017 | DDC 745.92/6—dc23
LC record available at https://lccn.loc.gov/2016032077

Originally published in hardcover as
*The Wreath Recipe Book* by Artisan in 2014

Design by Michelle Ishay-Cohen

Artisan books are available at special discounts when
purchased in bulk for premiums and sales promotions as
well as for fund-raising or educational use. Special editions
or book excerpts also can be created to specification. For
details, contact the Special Sales Director at the address
below, or send an e-mail to specialmarkets@workman.com.

Published by Artisan
A division of Workman Publishing Co., Inc.
225 Varick Street
New York, NY 10014-4381
artisanbooks.com

Artisan is a registered trademark of
Workman Publishing Co., Inc.

Published simultaneously in Canada by
Thomas Allen & Son, Limited

Printed in China
First printing, February 2016

10  9  8  7  6  5  4  3  2  1

*To all the people who help us every day*

# CONTENTS

# INTRODUCTION

Arrangements made from flowering branches announce that the seasons are changing, today is special, and good things are on their way. They help us celebrate day-to-day living and bring the outdoors into our homes. You don't need a reason to drape a garland over your mantel or hang a wreath on your front door, and you don't need any fancy supplies, either. Cuttings from a recent pruning of your apple tree or sprigs collected on a family hike are all you need to make personal pieces to decorate your space.

## HOW IT WORKS

We've assembled collections of ingredients, each one including a branch that is representative of a season (think springtime cherry branches or boughs of wintry pine), then created a family of flowers, foliage, and flair around them. The branches aren't featured in every project but are used as a jumping-off point to highlight the other ingredients within the collection. They are presented first as a still life (a lovely tabletop vignette in itself), followed by a set of projects of varying complexity.

Projects include:

**Wreaths** and **swags**, which make beautiful displays on doors or walls. A trio of small and simple wreaths hung together can be just as impactful as a large and complicated arrangement. Freshen up your home by removing a picture from your wall and replacing it with a dramatic handmade statement piece.

**Garlands**, which are traditionally placed over mantels or running down railings. Drape them over doorways or entryways, or wind one down the center of a table for a low-lying centerpiece. We like hanging garlands on the back of the guest of honor's chair, or on a bare wall to create a fun photo backdrop.

**Place settings** or **napkin rings**, something small and sweet to greet guests as they sit down to dinner. You can use one to dress up a special package or group a series to create a centerpiece.

**Centerpieces** and **focal arrangements**, versatile arrangements that should be sized to best suit your needs. Centerpieces are usually low, so they are out of the way when guests are reaching and talking. Focal arrangements are personality pieces with more height and angles and are best placed in areas where they can shine yet won't snag passersby.

Since building wreaths requires a slightly different set of skills and tools than creating arrangements, we've provided separate sections about each that lay out the important tools and techniques.

### SEASON TO TASTE

This book provides you with recipes, but unlike when you're cooking, these recipes are only guidelines—there's really no risk of ruining the batch. We've chosen the ingredients based on the seasonality, true, but we've also based the ingredients on what we like. If you hate persimmons, don't use them. If you want to add ten stems of narcissus instead of three, go for it.

### GIVE YOURSELF SOME LEEWAY

Sometimes it may make more sense for a branch to arc to one side rather than the other, so don't hesitate to make alterations to the overall composition as you see fit. Keep in mind that all branches are different, and they come in many shapes and sizes. Consider the arcs of your stems and the flexibility of your branches; while you can try to re-create the looks here, it's more important that you work with what you've got to make something you like.

### MAKE IT YOUR OWN

The plant world is immense, and the combinations you can create are almost infinite. We encourage you to find seasonal combinations of your own and work your own magic. Everyone should have a signature dish, so consider this book the first step to finding your signature wreath or garland.

# GOOD TO KNOW

## SOURCING INGREDIENTS

A good relationship with your local florist or nursery will do wonders for your projects. The staff will let you know what's in season and how flowers hold up over time or out of water, can help you track down your ingredients, and are generally a fount of useful information. In addition to the ingredients found in commercial and retail outlets, some great materials are sitting in your backyard as we speak.

Better yet, forage for the future by creating a simple drying rack. A spring and summer bounty of ingredients dried for future use will help you when autumn and winter arrive.

## WORKING WITH THE SEASONS

As when cooking, gathering your ingredients will be easier if you shop with the seasons. It's hard to find a good batch of corn in January, so you wait until June when there will be plenty of good-quality ears to choose from. There will always be some wiggle room between seasons, so pay attention to the availability of flowers and branches in your region.

We live in Northern California, where winters are warmer and summers are cooler than in many other places in the United States. Most of our ingredients are sourced from the warmer, western regions, and there is no doubt that some people will have a hard time finding them in their area or will have a different bloom time. Don't be disheartened. If you're desperate for an ingredient that you can't find, contact your local nursery or florist and find out if there are comparable materials available, or go ahead and place a special order.

## SUBSTITUTIONS

Be aware of an ingredient's limitations, such as flexibility if you're replacing one branch for another in a wrapped wreath project, or how long your substitutes can last out of water (they may need a water tube).

## PLACEMENT

When hanging wreaths or garlands in a room, it's important to think about how the room will be used. If it will be filled with people in tight quarters, it is probably best to keep your projects and arrangements out of high-traffic areas. If a garland takes up too much valuable real estate on a mantel, try draping it over an entryway instead. For materials that have a habit of dropping as time goes by (such as needles or berries), avoid placing them where they may get bumped or fall into food.

## TOXICITY

Many of the projects we work on in this book incorporate branches with fruits and berries, some of which are toxic and all of which should be kept out of reach of children and pets. Take into account that berries may fall from branches, so make sure that wherever they land, they are out of harm's way.

# THE ANATOMY OF A BRANCH

The great thing about working with branches is that one goes a long way. A single branch can yield several usable pieces, so you have enough leftovers to make another project. These are the different parts of a branch that we refer to throughout this book.

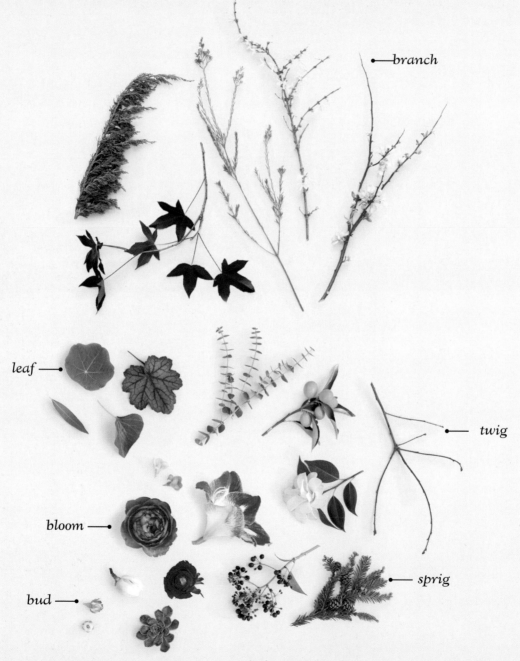

branch

leaf

twig

bloom

sprig

bud

# BRANCH CUTTING TECHNIQUES

When **cutting down branches**, it's best to make your cuts at locations where you will end up with pieces that have a good number of buds, leaves, berries, or fruits. Look for natural "breaks" at which to cut, usually located where the branch forks. **Sectional cutting** is used throughout this book for breaking down branches into manageable parts.

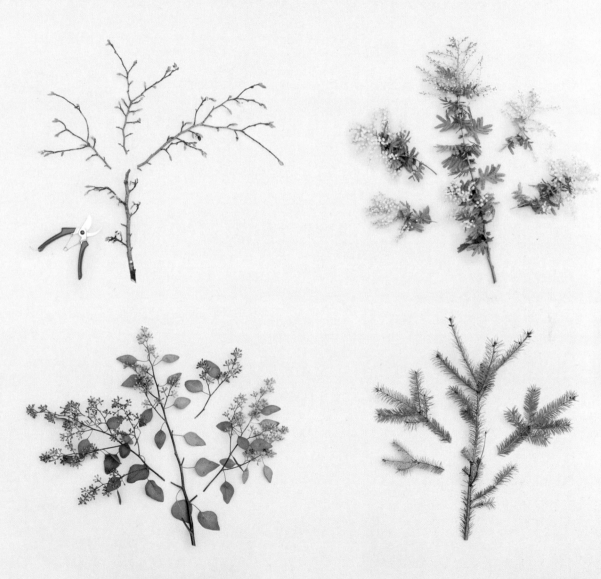

# WREATHS AND GARLANDS

When it comes to making wreaths, it's pretty easy to make a gourmet-looking one with a humble pantry of ingredients. Wreaths (and garlands and swags, too) are forgiving, flexible, and fun. When building an arrangement, a stem cut too short may quickly unravel your plans, but wreaths and garlands make it easy to work with what you've got even when mistakes are made. Trim something too short? Tuck it, wire it—whatever you do, there's no wrong place to put it in a wreath.

Wreaths and garlands are built in this book in very similar ways; the difference between a wreath and a garland in most cases is the difference between a circle and a line. Both are made by attaching ingredients to a frame or base, either by using the continuous-wrap technique or by wiring pieces individually.

A technique we refer to again and again in the wreath and garland projects is called gathering, and it's where the real designing comes in. With each bundle, you are creating a little bouquet or arrangement, but once you wire it to your project, it is literally and figuratively out of your hands—a bundle wired to a project is difficult to remove. Take time to design and build your bundles. As always, figure out the personality of the ingredients you want to highlight, then choose the frame or base that will work best.

# WREATHING TOOLS

## FRAMES AND BASES

**Grapevine frames** are readily available at most craft stores. These frames are sturdy, look good left exposed, and are great for tucking stems into.

**Honeysuckle frames** are less rigid and more malleable than grapevine frames, yet are also great for tucking and look fantastic exposed. Honeysuckle typically comes in a large roll and can be cut apart to make wreaths of various sizes.

**Single wire frames** can either be covered completely by your ingredients or left exposed in places for a light, streamlined look.

**Double-ring wire frames** are sturdy workhorses that are not pliable and are usually covered completely by ingredients.

**Branches** (not pictured) are great natural bases for garlands, wall hangings, and mobiles, in addition to their use on tabletops for centerpiece arrangements.

**Log slices** with a wire driven into the center create the perfect display base for a single stem or a piece of fruit.

## SECURING

**Twine** is a natural fiber string that comes in handy for a variety of projects.

**Heavy-gauge wire** (10–16 gauge) is used to skewer dense ingredients, to secure heavy items to a frame, and in log-slice projects.

**Medium-gauge wire** (18–26 gauge) is an all-purpose wire and is used to attach ingredients to wreath frames and bases.

**Thin-gauge wire** (28–32 gauge) is used to attach more delicate items to lightweight frames and bases.

**Paddle wire** is used for continuous wrapping. As ingredients are added to a base or frame, it is wrapped around each new piece without being cut until all ingredients have been added.

**Bind wire** is a paper-coated wire that prevents ingredients from slipping when attached to frames.

**Fishing line** is a clear filament string that works to suspend light objects, creating the illusion of ingredients floating in midair.

**Floral glue** is an adhesive used to attach flowers and leaves to surfaces, and to secure objects on skewers.

## ADDITIONS

**Ribbon** and **cord** are used as decorative elements and to hang finished projects.

**Thread** and **embroidery floss** are used to hang and secure lighter elements, and for wrapping branches.

**Spray paint** adds an unexpected pop of color to leaves and branches.

**Feathers**, **pinecones**, and **moss** are natural elements that add depth and texture to projects.

## TOOLS AND OTHER SUPPLIES

**Floral snips** are used to trim nonwoody stems and flower heads from stems.

**Pruners** are used to cut the woody stems of branches and flowers.

**Water tubes** are placed on cut stems to keep flowers hydrated.

**Needles** are available in various sizes and are used to thread ingredients onto a string.

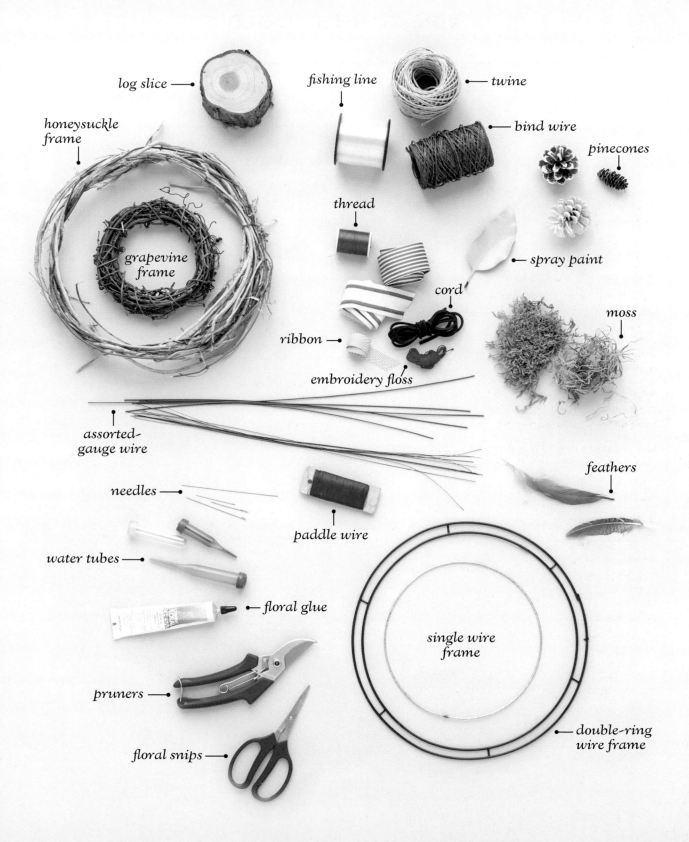

log slice

fishing line

twine

honeysuckle frame

bind wire

pinecones

grapevine frame

thread

spray paint

cord

ribbon

moss

embroidery floss

assorted-gauge wire

feathers

needles

paddle wire

water tubes

floral glue

single wire frame

pruners

double-ring wire frame

floral snips

# ATTACHMENT TECHNIQUES

WIRING is a way to attach a piece of fruit, a flower, a leaf, or another object to a project. A straight wire can be wrapped around an object or stem, or threaded through the base, then secured in place by twisting the wire around the back side of the project.

**SKEWERING FRUIT** adds a "stem" to an ingredient that has none, allowing it to be easily tucked into a wreath. Place a drop of floral glue on the fruit, then drive a wooden skewer through the drop of glue and into the fruit, being careful not to go all the way through. The glue will create a seal and secure the skewer in place. Allow the glue to dry before tucking the skewered ingredient into a wreath.

**TRIMMING BLOOMS** allows them to be wired to a wreath, or threaded and added to a garland. Be careful not to trim the bloom too short or the petals will separate from one another: Make your cut just below the receptacle that holds each bloom together.

**STRINGING FLOWERS** on thread, embroidery floss, or fishing line is one of the easier ways to create a quick and simple garland. Thread a needle with string, and cut it to the desired length. Run the threaded needle through the center of the ingredients, pulling them down as you continue adding. **Stringing fruit** requires a longer, heavier needle and heavier-gauge string but follows the same technique as stringing flowers. If you find that the needle is difficult to push or pull through the fruit, then—exercising caution—use a piece of scrap wood to apply downward pressure on the needle to drive it through the center.

# HYDRATION TECHNIQUES

**BAGGING** is a way to keep delicate ingredients hydrated when a water tube would damage the stem; it also allows you to use multiple stems when tubes would prove too bulky or impractical. Wrap several stems together in a wet paper towel. Place the wrapped stems in a small plastic bag, add a small amount of water, and secure it with a rubber band. The package can then be wired onto a wreath or garland, with the foliage concealing the bag.

**WATER TUBES** can be added to stems that have a short shelf life out of water. Start by filling a water tube a little more than halfway. Make an angled cut on your stem, then insert it into the water tube, making sure the stem is in the water. We refer to this technique as "trim and tube" throughout the book. Water tubes can leak when upside down, so check placement when finalizing your project. Flowers and branches are thirsty, so tubes will need to be refilled frequently!

# BUILDING A GARLAND, STEP-BY-STEP

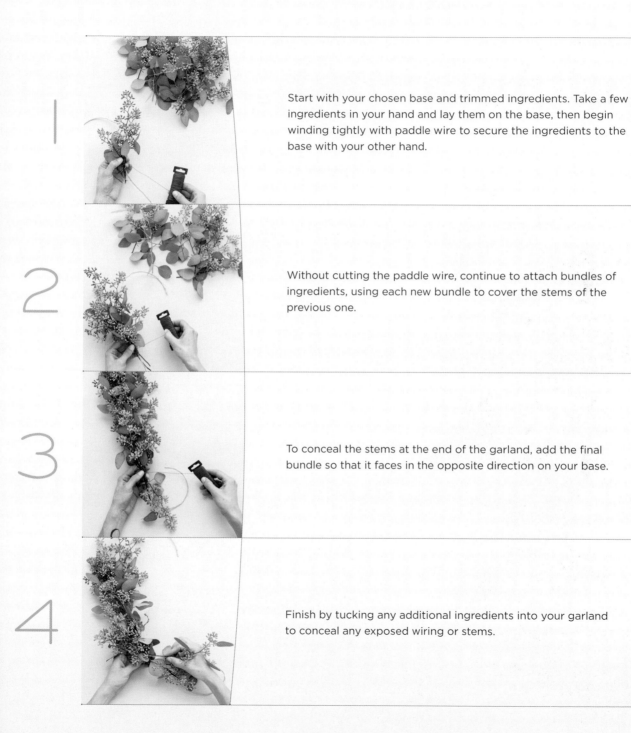

**1** Start with your chosen base and trimmed ingredients. Take a few ingredients in your hand and lay them on the base, then begin winding tightly with paddle wire to secure the ingredients to the base with your other hand.

**2** Without cutting the paddle wire, continue to attach bundles of ingredients, using each new bundle to cover the stems of the previous one.

**3** To conceal the stems at the end of the garland, add the final bundle so that it faces in the opposite direction on your base.

**4** Finish by tucking any additional ingredients into your garland to conceal any exposed wiring or stems.

# BUILDING A WREATH, STEP-BY-STEP

1    Start with your chosen frame and ingredients. Using sectional cutting, trim the ingredients into smaller sections or sprigs.

2    Assemble a bundle of ingredients in your hand in a pleasing composition. Remember that this is where you're doing most of your designing, so take your time to arrange each bundle.

3    Hold the bundle against the frame with one hand, and use paddle wire to secure the bundle to the frame with your other hand, wrapping it around several times. Wrap tightly enough so that the ingredients hold but not so tightly that the wire breaks.

4    Without cutting the paddle wire, continue to make bundles of ingredients and attach them to the frame, working around the entire frame, using each new bundle to cover the stems of the previous one.

5    Continue adding bundles around the frame.

6    Tuck the last bundle's stems underneath the foliage of the first bundle, wrapping several times. Then cut the wire and tuck the end into the wreath so it won't scratch the wall or door when the wreath is hung.

7    Finish by tucking any additional ingredients into your wreath at pleasing locations or to cover exposed stems or wires.

8    Before hanging, fluff and prune the ingredients as needed.

# ARRANGEMENTS

Although the focus of this book is on wreaths, garlands, and other special-occasion projects, we couldn't leave arrangements out in the cold. Of course, if you find yourself wanting to go more in-depth with arrangements, then definitely check out our first book, *The Flower Recipe Book,* to get your fix.

Bunches of branches always look beautiful on their own in a tall vase, but we encourage you to experiment with lots of different combinations. Don't be afraid to create airy arrangements with a single branch or to try a long and low draping display. Make arrangements that highlight your favorite part of the branch, be it an interesting sweeping arc or a colorful cluster of foliage.

Along with the recipes, the still-life openers are meant to be used as additional arranging projects. They show how to create a cohesive display using separate vessels with a single ingredient type in each. The style of vases and vessels is kept simple to emphasize the ingredients and how they work together.

{ 23 }

# SUPPLIES

## VASES AND VESSELS

A **medium-sized bowl** is good for low arrangements when outfitted with chicken wire or a flower frog.

A **tall vase** with a hefty weight is essential for creating arrangements with height and to highlight long, beautiful branches.

**Small bud vases** can hold individual arrangements or single blooms; several can work together to make place settings and centerpieces.

## SECURING

**Floral tape** is lightweight and becomes sticky when stretched, making it ideal for locking a carefully arranged bundle of ingredients into place.

**Waterproof tape** is used to secure chicken wire frames into vessels.

**Chicken wire** is used to stabilize stems in an arrangement, especially in wide vases and vessels.

**Wooden skewers** are driven through fruit and other ingredients (see page 17), creating artificial "stems" so they can easily be added to projects.

**Floral glue** secures skewers in place and can attach flowers and other ingredients to a variety of surfaces.

**Rubber bands** are used to gather small bundles of ingredients when they need to be tightly clustered.

**Flower frogs** are used to stabilize stems in arrangements.

**Floral putty** is used to secure a flower frog to the bottom of a vase to keep it from shifting.

## TOOLS

**Floral snips** are for trimming stems, cleaning, and making angled and sectional cuttings.

**Pruners** are used for making woody cuts and trimming thicker stems and branches for arrangements.

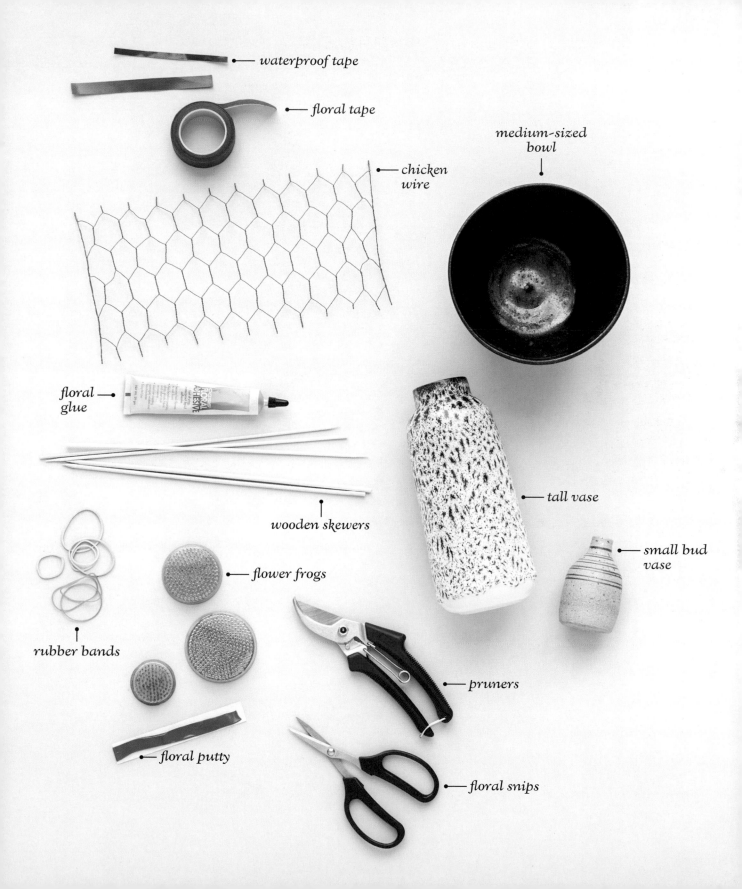

waterproof tape

floral tape

chicken wire

medium-sized bowl

floral glue

wooden skewers

tall vase

small bud vase

rubber bands

flower frogs

floral putty

pruners

floral snips

# STEM CARE

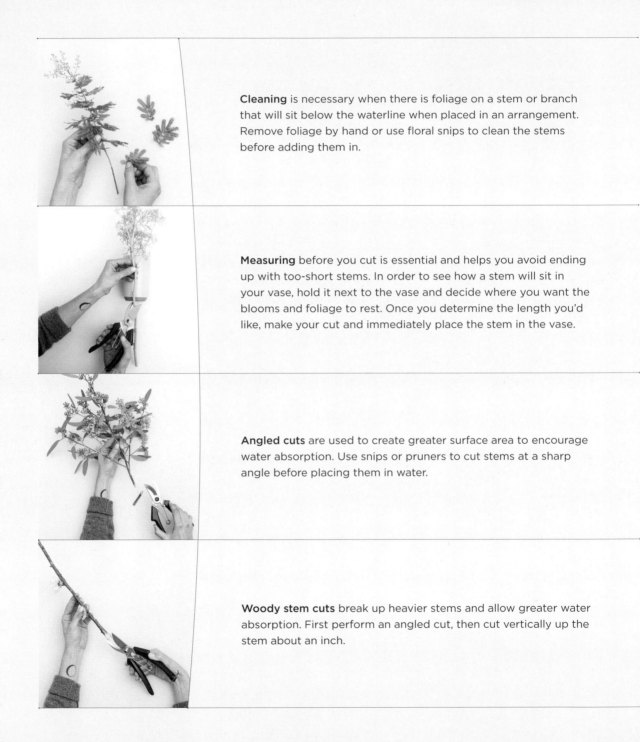

**Cleaning** is necessary when there is foliage on a stem or branch that will sit below the waterline when placed in an arrangement. Remove foliage by hand or use floral snips to clean the stems before adding them in.

**Measuring** before you cut is essential and helps you avoid ending up with too-short stems. In order to see how a stem will sit in your vase, hold it next to the vase and decide where you want the blooms and foliage to rest. Once you determine the length you'd like, make your cut and immediately place the stem in the vase.

**Angled cuts** are used to create greater surface area to encourage water absorption. Use snips or pruners to cut stems at a sharp angle before placing them in water.

**Woody stem cuts** break up heavier stems and allow greater water absorption. First perform an angled cut, then cut vertically up the stem about an inch.

# ARRANGING TECHNIQUES

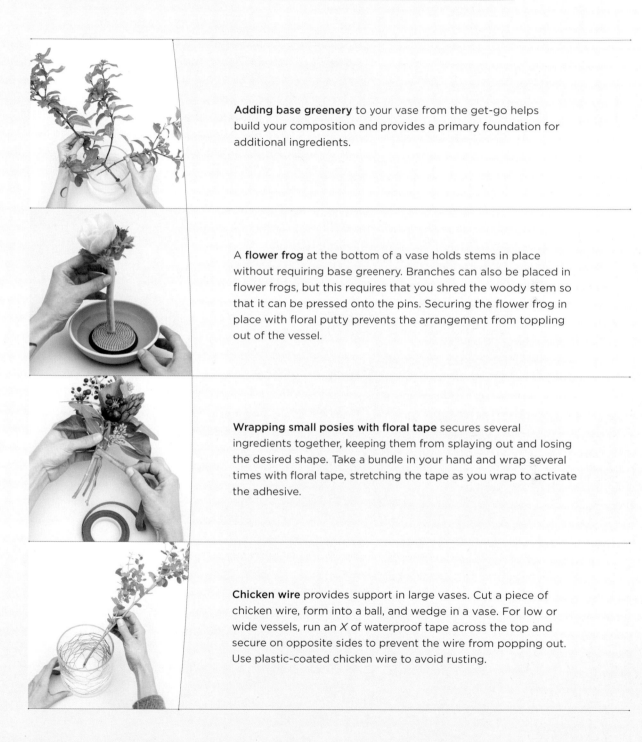

**Adding base greenery** to your vase from the get-go helps build your composition and provides a primary foundation for additional ingredients.

A **flower frog** at the bottom of a vase holds stems in place without requiring base greenery. Branches can also be placed in flower frogs, but this requires that you shred the woody stem so that it can be pressed onto the pins. Securing the flower frog in place with floral putty prevents the arrangement from toppling out of the vessel.

**Wrapping small posies with floral tape** secures several ingredients together, keeping them from splaying out and losing the desired shape. Take a bundle in your hand and wrap several times with floral tape, stretching the tape as you wrap to activate the adhesive.

**Chicken wire** provides support in large vases. Cut a piece of chicken wire, form into a ball, and wedge in a vase. For low or wide vessels, run an *X* of waterproof tape across the top and secure on opposite sides to prevent the wire from popping out. Use plastic-coated chicken wire to avoid rusting.

SPRING

# CHERRY BLOSSOM

Celebrated at cherry blossom festivals all over the world, these branches are plentiful and easy to find in most regions throughout the spring and should last for 2 weeks in water. The papery petals of cherry blossoms, sweet peas, and godetia combine beautifully to create wonderfully fluffy, light-as-air arrangements. All of these blooms bring out the happy and playful colors that we associate with spring.

*cherry blossom*

*sweet pea*

*godetia*

# RECIPE 1:
## CENTERPIECE

——————

### INGREDIENTS
1 cherry branch

5 stems of godetia

3 stems of sweet pea

### MATERIALS
Small cup

Flower frog

Floral putty

**Gather the best bits from a cherry branch and pair them with delicate godetia and sweet peas.**

1.  Place the flower frog in the bottom of the cup and secure with floral putty. Trim a few sprigs from the cherry branch and add them to the left side of the cup.

2.  Trim and add the stems of godetia to the right side so that the blooms rest at the rim.

3.  Trim and add the stems of sweet pea above the godetia to create the highest point in the arrangement.

# RECIPE 2:
## FOCAL ARRANGEMENT

---

### INGREDIENTS

5 cherry branches

### MATERIALS

Tall, narrow vase

Large garbage bag

Painter's tape

Fluorescent-pink
spray paint

**A few branches of cherry blossoms become a piece of art with a little paint and planning.**

1.  Trim the cherry branches and add them to the vase in a pleasing arrangement.

2.  Place the vase in the garbage bag, leaving only the branches exposed. Secure the garbage bag to the neck of the vase with painter's tape.

3.  Spray the branches with the spray paint, starting from the neck of the vase and working up until you've sprayed approximately 12 inches of the branches. Reapply paint as necessary to reach the desired opacity.

4.  Wait until the paint has completely dried, then remove the painter's tape and garbage bag from the vase.

# RECIPE 3:
## WALL HANGING

---

### INGREDIENTS
1 cherry branch

### MATERIALS
1 yard of ribbon

3 assorted ribbons,
in ½-, 1-, and
2-yard lengths

Trim the cherry branch at the point where the blooms begin, and attach the 1-yard-long ribbon to two points in the middle of the branch.

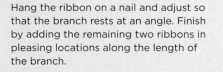

2 Hang the ribbon on a nail and adjust so that the branch rests at an angle. Finish by adding the remaining two ribbons in pleasing locations along the length of the branch.

For this easy project, be sure to choose a cherry branch filled with amazing blossoms—the more blossoms, the better. Colorful pieces of ribbon add a touch of whimsy.

crab apple

Ammi

hellebore

# CRAB APPLE

Unlike the apples that are harvested for food (making the branches a rare find at the flower stand), the bitter fruit of the crab apple makes them more desirable for arrangements. The combination of country crab apple and tropical orchids may not make sense on paper, but together with a few exotic hellebores, they create a surprisingly cohesive and interesting group. Look for a crab apple branch with unopened buds for a longer life, and expect flowers to hold on for about 5 days after blooming.

*ti leaf*

*mini cymbidium orchid*

{ 37 }

# RECIPE 1:
## CENTERPIECE

---

### INGREDIENTS

10 hellebore blooms

10 mini cymbidium orchids

### MATERIALS

Shallow bowl

**A shallow bowl holding hellebore and mini cymbidium orchid blooms can last for weeks with little to no attention.**

1. Place a small amount of water in the bowl.

2. Place the flower heads faceup in the bowl, arranging so that the blooms cover the entire surface area.

CRAB APPLE
## RECIPE 2:
FOCAL
ARRANGEMENT

———

### INGREDIENTS

5 branches of crab
apple

5 stems of *Ammi*

3 stems of hellebore

### MATERIALS

Medium vase

These unwieldy arms might be too much for a sit-down dinner, so use this arrangement as a focal piece on a side table or credenza.

1.  Trim and add the crab apple branches to the vase so that the shorter branches extend to the left and the longer branches extend toward the right.

2.  Trim the stems of *Ammi* to various heights and cluster throughout the arrangement, adding longer stems to the left side to mirror the crab apple on the right.

3.  Trim and add the stems of hellebore in a cluster in the middle of the arrangement.

Trim and tube two branches
of crab apple and lay them
on the display surface.

2  Add two ti leaves on top of the branches,
covering the tubed end.

3  Lay one piece of the mini cymbidium
orchid on top of the ti leaf.

4  Repeat with the remaining ingredients,
taking care to cover the water tubes.

This simply laid "garland" is the perfect low-profile centerpiece for a long table. Orchids and ti leaves add earthy tones that keep the pink crab apple blooms from being too precious.

dogwood

mushroom

fritillaria

# DOGWOOD

With its simple, curled petals and spare foliage, there's something almost primitive about dogwood. Pair these big, blooming branches with the rough mosses, lichens, and loamy mushrooms that appear after a heavy spring rain. Fritillaria, another forest dweller, adds a bit of color and complexity to the mix. Expect a good branch of dogwood to hold its flowers for at least a week in water.

*fritillaria*

*mushroom*

*assorted mosses and lichen*

# RECIPE 1:
## FOCAL ARRANGEMENT

---

### INGREDIENTS

1 branch of dogwood

5 stems of fritillaria

Assorted mushrooms

### MATERIALS

Medium low bowl

Flower frog

Floral putty

Bring a bit of the forest floor to your tabletop with this earthy display. Mushrooms are very absorbent and will suck up all your arrangement's water overnight, so it's best to make this a one-night engagement.

1. Place the flower frog in the bottom of the bowl and secure with floral putty. Trim the branch of dogwood and place it securely in the frog toward the back of the bowl.

2. Trim and add the two tallest fritillaria to the left side of the arrangement in front of the dogwood, then trim the remaining three fritillaria, adding them in a cluster on the right side.

3. Fill in the base of the arrangement with the assorted mushrooms to conceal the flower frog.

DOGWOOD
# RECIPE 2:
GARLAND

————

## INGREDIENTS
Assorted mushrooms

Assorted mosses
and lichen

## MATERIALS
String

Embroidery needle

Lacy lichen and chunky mushrooms appear to float in the air when strung on a thin string. The elements of this project will be vibrant the first day, and will slowly dry over time.

1. Using the embroidery needle, thread the string through various pieces of mushrooms, moss, and lichen, alternating different colors and textures.

2. Space each piece 1 to 2 inches apart along the garland until you achieve the desired length.

## DOGWOOD
# RECIPE 3:
## WREATH

———

### INGREDIENTS

2 branches of
dogwood

One 6-by-6-inch
piece of sheet moss

10 assorted
mushrooms

Several pieces of lichen

### MATERIALS

2 water tubes

Thin-gauge wire

Heavy-gauge wire

1 | Trim and tube the branches of dogwood.

2 | Bend each branch around in a loop and attach the loops together with thin-gauge wire to create a frame.

3 | Scrunch the sheet moss around the base of the loop so that the wire and tubes are no longer visible.

4 | Hang the wreath in place before adding the mushrooms. Stake several mushrooms with heavy-gauge wire and add them to the moss patch. Finish by tucking in pieces of lichen.

The woody, flexible branches of flowering dogwood frame a whimsical vignette that can last up to 2 weeks when the water tubes are kept filled.

# FORSYTHIA

Forsythia's electric-yellow flowers are its standout char-
acteristic, and a family of ferns adds greenery that the
branch itself lacks. A tiny touch of blue from the diminutive muscari complements the intense yellows of this
group, leaving no doubt that spring has finally arrived.
The flowers on a forsythia branch can last for a few weeks
if kept in a cool spot.

*sword fern*

*maidenhair fern*

*plumosa fern*

*forsythia*

*daffodil*

*muscari*

---

### INGREDIENTS

10 stems of muscari

1 daffodil

8 fronds of
maidenhair fern

### MATERIALS

2 small, low bowls

2 flower frogs

Floral putty

Delicate maidenhair ferns provide a perfect resting spot for tiny muscari and a single daffodil. Add multiple arrangements down a long table to create the impression of a wandering woodland path.

1. Place the flower frogs in the bottoms of the bowls and secure with floral putty.

2. Trim and add the stems of muscari to one bowl so that the blooms sit a few inches above the rim; then trim and add five fronds of maidenhair fern.

3. Trim and add the daffodil to the other bowl so that the bloom rests on the rim; then trim and add the remaining three fronds of maidenhair fern.

FORSYTHIA
# RECIPE 2:
## WREATH

————

**INGREDIENTS**

2 fronds of
plumosa fern

**MATERIALS**

12-inch piece of ribbon

Thin-gauge wire

**Hang a simple wreath of plumosa fern on an unadorned wall to highlight the wispiness of this fragile fern.**

1. Use thin-gauge wire to attach the tip of one frond of plumosa fern to the stem of the other.

2. Form the connected ferns into a circle and attach the remaining tip and stem.

3. Finish by tying the ribbon to the top of the wreath.

# RECIPE 3:
## FOCAL ARRANGEMENT

---

### INGREDIENTS
6 branches of forsythia

2 fronds of plumosa fern

### MATERIALS
Bind wire

Large, shallow bowl

**Take advantage of forsythia's flexibility by bending it into an unexpected low-lying centerpiece.**

1. At the most flexible point of a forsythia branch, bend the end around to meet its base. Create a teardrop shape, securing the ends together with bind wire. Repeat with the remaining five branches.

2. Trim each teardrop loop several inches below the wire connection.

3. Stack the loops in the bowl in alternating directions, overlapping the wired ends to create a figure-eight pattern. Make sure the trimmed ends are in the water.

4. Trim and tuck the fronds of plumosa fern into the center where the loops overlap, cascading the long fronds so that they extend down the display surface.

# FORSYTHIA
# RECIPE 4:
## GARLAND

————

### INGREDIENTS

10 fronds of
maidenhair fern

10 fronds of sword fern

10 fronds of
plumosa fern

### MATERIALS

Bind wire

Paddle wire

1 | Cut a piece of bind wire to
the desired length for your
garland, leaving several extra
inches for hanging. Make a
loop at one end.

2 Lay a fern on the end of the bind wire
so that it hides the loop. Wrap paddle
wire around the stem and the bind wire
several times to secure it in place.

3 Gather a small bundle of assorted ferns
and place it on top of the first fern,
covering its stem. Wrap paddle wire
around the base of the bundle and the
bind wire several times.

4 Continue making and attaching fern
bundles down the length of the garland.
Make a loop at the end of the bind wire.
Attach the last bundle of ferns in the
opposite direction on the garland so that
it hides the loop.

The delicate fronds of several different types
of ferns fan out from this garland, emphasizing
their feathery silhouettes.

# LILAC

Lilac's fragrant flowers form puffs of purple atop sturdy branches, making it the perfect candidate for pieces both small and large. Feathery agonis leaves, polished olives, and a spiky, spiny air plant create a texturally impressive palette. Lilac blooms are not known for their longevity (expect them to last about a week indoors), but a cool place, plenty of water, and a fresh cut every day will help prevent wilting.

lilac

air plant

*agonis*

*olive branch*

*berzelia*

LILAC
# RECIPE 1:
## PLACE SETTING

---

### INGREDIENTS

2 sprigs of olive

2 stems of berzelia

1 small air plant

### MATERIALS

Floral tape

12-inch piece of ribbon

A small bundle of unexpected elements is the perfect way to welcome guests to their dinner plate. It's also a lovely touch atop a simple, craft-paper–wrapped package. This little posy will last for several days without water.

1. Gather the olive sprigs and stems of berzelia.

2. Secure by wrapping the stems with floral tape just below the foliage. Tie on the ribbon, making sure to cover the floral tape.

3. Trim the stems to about an inch below the ribbon, and finish by tucking the air plant just above the ribbon.

LILAC

# RECIPE 2:
## GARLAND

———

**INGREDIENTS**

4 olive branches

**MATERIALS**

Bind wire

Paddle wire

**Olive branches make the perfect table runner for a dinner party, particularly if Italian food is on the menu.**

1. Cut a piece of bind wire to the desired length for your garland. Using sectional cutting (see page 11), trim the olive branches into sprigs that are 4 to 6 inches long.

2. Lay a sprig of olive on the end of the bind wire. Wrap paddle wire around the stem and the bind wire several times to secure it in place.

3. Continue attaching the remaining sprigs down the length of the garland, tucking in the last one in the opposite direction on the garland.

# RECIPE 3:
## FOCAL ARRANGEMENT

---

### INGREDIENTS
3 lilac branches

### MATERIALS
Widemouthed bowl

Flower frog

Floral putty

Embroidery thread in assorted colors

The two sides of lilac's personality (woody/strong and fluffy/fragrant) are best appreciated when the branches are left long and natural.

1. Place the flower frog in the bottom of the bowl and secure with floral putty.

2. Wrap bare sections of each branch in several different colors of embroidery thread. Tie and trim the thread so that long pieces drape and puddle at the base of the arrangement.

3. Trim and add the lilac branches to the vase so that the threads are visible and the branches don't overlap.

# RECIPE 4:
## WREATH

---

### INGREDIENTS

5 olive branches

10 blooms of lilac

6 stems of agonis

2 stems of berzelia

2 air plants

### MATERIALS

Grapevine wreath frame

5 water tubes

Medium-gauge wire

Start with the grapevine wreath frame.

2  Tuck the olive branches into the top and bottom of the frame so that the ends point to the right.

3  Trim and add two blooms of lilac to each filled water tube. Place the lilacs in clusters around the wreath and secure with medium-gauge wire.

4  Tuck the stems of agonis and berzelia around the lilac clusters to conceal the water tubes. Finish by attaching the air plants to the bottom of the wreath.

Welcome guests to your party before they even walk through the door with a fragrance-forward wreath. Although the lilacs on this wreath will last only one night, the rest of the ingredients will dry nicely over time.

# QUINCE

Quince is one of the earliest-blooming spring branches; there is still a serious chill in the air when these blossoms start to appear. Since quince blooms right on the heels of the winter citrus season, there's plenty of pretty fruit around to complement its sculptural, thorny branches. Look for branches with unopened buds, which can last up to 3 weeks in water. Tip: The leathery green leaves of salal can be used to mimic citrus leaves.

*ranunculus*

*salal*

*rosemary*

quince

kumquat

QUINCE
# RECIPE 1:
## PLACE SETTING

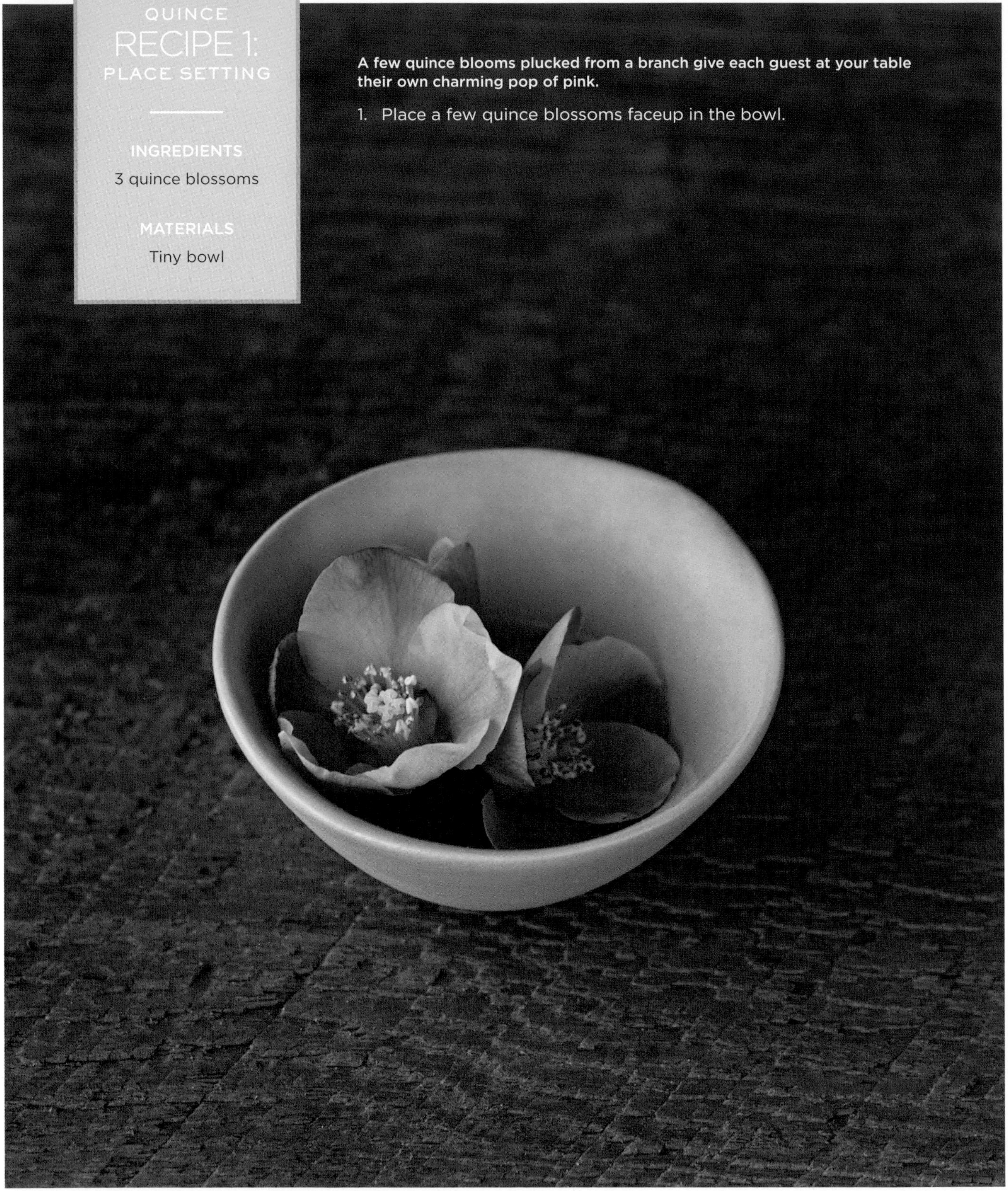

**INGREDIENTS**

3 quince blossoms

**MATERIALS**

Tiny bowl

**A few quince blooms plucked from a branch give each guest at your table their own charming pop of pink.**

1. Place a few quince blossoms faceup in the bowl.

QUINCE
## RECIPE 2:
FOCAL
ARRANGEMENT

————

### INGREDIENTS

1 quince branch

3 branches of kumquat

3 stems of salal

3 stems of rosemary

5 stems of ranunculus

### MATERIALS

Medium bowl

Flower frog

Floral putty

**A plentiful arrangement of fruit, flowers, and powerful fragrances is a welcome reminder that springtime is here.**

1. Place the flower frog in the bottom of the bowl and secure with floral putty. Trim and add the quince branch so that it arcs out dramatically on the left side.

2. Trim and add the branches of kumquat so that they rest in clusters at the rim in the center and on the right.

3. Fill in the empty spaces around the kumquat by trimming and adding the three stems of salal and two stems of rosemary.

4. Trim and add the ranunculus to the middle of the arrangement, layering the blooms between the citrus clusters. Finish by trimming and adding the remaining stem of rosemary to the back right side of the arrangement to balance the quince on the left.

QUINCE
# RECIPE 3:
WREATH

———

### INGREDIENTS
Dried honeysuckle
vines

1 quince branch

4 stems of salal

2 branches of kumquat

### MATERIALS
Medium-gauge wire

Water tube

1 | Form a bundle of honeysuckle vines into a crescent shape, securing with medium-gauge wire at the top and bottom.

2 | Trim and tube the quince branch and lay it diagonally across the wreath. Secure it in place at the top and bottom with wire.

3 | Tuck in the stems of salal around the wreath, making sure to hide the water tube.

4 | Add the branches of kumquat, tucking them in and securing with wire. Hang with a support at the top and at the bottom of the wreath.

Take advantage of the citrus fruit that late winter has to offer by combining it with newly bloomed branches to create a wreath that bridges the seasons.

# SPIREA

Spirea is a branch that might get overlooked because of its tiny flowers and diminutive leaves. A little unwieldy and unrefined at times, here spirea is paired with a few traditional ingredients to accentuate its wild ways. The tiny waxflower and roses add a strong hit of color and stand out in a sea of green and white foliage. Although spirea doesn't have a long shelf life, the other elements are hardy and long-lasting.

*spirea*

*rose*

*pittosporum*

*waxflower*

*spirea*

# RECIPE 1:
## PLACE SETTING

---

### INGREDIENTS
1 rose

2 sprigs of pittosporum

1 sprig of waxflower

### MATERIALS
Floral tape

12-inch piece of ribbon

**Set out a petite posy and pin for each guest to make them feel special.**

1.  Gather the rose, pittosporum, and waxflower.

2.  Secure by wrapping with floral tape just below the blooms.

3.  Tie on the ribbon, making sure to cover the floral tape.

4.  Trim the stems to 2 inches below the ribbon.

### INGREDIENTS

7 spirea branches

5 pittosporum
branches

3 branches of
waxflower

### MATERIALS

Low wood box

Liner

Chicken wire,
cut to fit the box

Waterproof tape

**Bushy spirea fills in arrangements fast, and its fresh-from-the-field look
adds wild texture.**

1. Add the liner to the box to make it watertight. Form a rounded
   shape with the chicken wire and tape in place in the box to
   create a supportive structure for the arrangement.

2. Trim and add the tallest spirea branches to the middle of the
   chicken wire grid, and continue to add the smaller pieces to
   both sides.

3. Trim and add the pittosporum branches to the center of the
   arrangement to fill in any open spaces.

4. Finish by trimming and adding the branches of waxflower to
   the center.

Trim and tube the
spirea branches.

2 Tightly wire the branches together,
end to end, so that the foliage from
each branch covers the water tube
of the other.

3 Lay the spigs of waxflower (facing in the
opposite direction) on top of the middle
of the spirea. Secure with wire.

4 Trim and tube the sprays of roses. Tuck
them in next to the waxflower and secure
with wire. To conceal the water tubes,
tuck in the branches of pittosporum.
Finish by adding the ribbon.

Two long, flowering branches of spirea create the perfect foundation for a dramatic swag, and a spray of pink garden roses adds a bit of rustic femininity. Keep the spirea water tubes filled to extend the life of this arrangement.

# TULIP TREE

When tulip trees bloom, their branches explode with exotic, fluorescent flowers. Their tight green buds hang unassumingly on branches until they open into colorful saucer-like blooms. The leaves of a variegated geranium mimic the shape and coloring of the tulip tree flower, while simple, streamlined tulips balance the intensity of this unique and prehistoric plant.

*geranium*

*lichen-covered branch*

*tulip tree*

*tulip*

*tulip*

TULIP TREE
# RECIPE 1:
## PLACE SETTING

———

### INGREDIENTS
3 tulip tree blooms

### MATERIALS
Small, shallow bowl

Small flower frog

Floral putty

The flowers of the tulip tree are usually lost overhead in big, leaf-covered branches. Pluck a few blooms and lay them in a shallow cup as a place setting so guests can appreciate their unique centers.

1. Place the flower frog in the bottom of the bowl and secure with floral putty.

2. Add the tulip tree blooms to the bowl so that they are facing in different directions.

---

### INGREDIENTS

5 tulips

Moss

### MATERIALS

Log slice

Heavy-gauge wire

Rubber band

**Thanks to some clever engineering and hidden hardware, a fountain of tulips appears to stand on its own.**

1. Cut a 4-inch piece of heavy-gauge wire and hammer it into the center of the log slice.

2. Gather the tulips into a pleasing composition. While holding the bunch, cut the stems all at once so that the bottom is even. Secure with the rubber band low on the base of the stems.

3. Place the banded tulips on top of the log slice so that the wire sticks up through the center and the bouquet stands upright on its own.

4. Add moss to conceal the rubber band.

# RECIPE 3:
### CENTERPIECE

---

### INGREDIENTS
2 lichen-covered sticks

2 tulip tree branches

Moss

### MATERIALS
Large flower frog

A few interesting branches displayed horizontally create a unique and inexpensive table runner. Tulip tree blooms are hardy and can last a day or two out of water.

1. Lay the lichen-covered sticks across the length of a display surface.

2. Place the flower frog between the sticks at the center point.

3. Add the first tulip tree branch to the frog, laying it horizontally so that the blooms face up and out. Add the remaining branch vertically to the frog to add height to the arrangement.

4. Conceal the frog with moss.

# TULIP TREE
# RECIPE 4:
## FOCAL ARRANGEMENT

———

### INGREDIENTS

2 tulip tree branches

3 stems of
geranium leaves

11 tulips

### MATERIALS

Large vase

1 | Select a vase heavy enough to support the weight of the tulip tree branches.

2 Trim and add the branches so that they lean over to the right side of the vase.

3 Trim and add the stems of geranium leaves to the left side of the arrangement so that the leaves rest right above the rim of the vase.

4 Trim and add five tulips to the left side of the arrangement. Finish by trimming adding the remaining six tulips to fill in the center and left side of the arrangement.

Take advantage of all the tulip tree has to offer by finding a branch with both blooming flowers and unopened buds for this high-reaching arrangement.

mock orange

viburnum

peony

# VIBURNUM

There's no ignoring the big, fluffy pom-poms of the viburnum tree when springtime comes around. Green and white are the dominant colors in this romantic collection that also features peony, parrot tulip, and mock orange. Viburnum blooms consist of tiny, simple florets and often retain a green hue when they first bloom. Expect flowers to last up to 5 days in water; nonfragrant varieties will have a slightly longer vase life.

*parrot tulip*

VIBURNUM
# RECIPE 1:
## PLACE SETTING

---

### INGREDIENTS
1 sprig of viburnum

1 stem of mock orange

1 parrot tulip

### MATERIALS
Floral tape

1 yard of ribbon

This place setting might have a short shelf life (expect it to last one evening), but the variety of shapes, sizes, and textures in this little posy makes a big impact.

1. Gather the viburnum, mock orange, and tulip.

2. Secure by wrapping with floral tape just below the blooms, and then tie on the ribbon, making sure to cover the tape.

3. Trim the stems to 3 inches below the ribbon.

## VIBURNUM
# RECIPE 2:
## GARLAND

——————

### INGREDIENTS
13 parrot tulips

### MATERIALS
Twine

Paddle wire

**Parrot tulips sometimes have droopy stems, which can make them difficult to arrange. Take advantage of their flexibility by wiring them into a cascading garland.**

1.  Cut a piece of twine to the desired length of your garland.

2.  Lay the first tulip on the twine, then wrap paddle wire around the stem and the twine several times to secure in place. Wrap tightly enough to firmly hold the stem in place but not so tightly that it slices through the tulip.

3.  Place the second tulip on top of the first, covering its stem, and wire it into place.

4.  Continue with the remaining tulips, alternating bloom direction to create a cascading shape.

### INGREDIENTS
3 viburnum branches

### MATERIALS
3 water tubes

Medium-gauge wire

**Using nothing but the simple beauty of the branch itself, this wreath is as close to standing underneath a viburnum tree as you can get without stepping outside.**

1. Trim and tube the viburnum branches.

2. Bend each branch into a loop and wire the tip to the tubed end. Repeat until you have created three loops of viburnum.

3. Stack the three loops on top of each other so that the viburnum blooms are clustered together, concealing the water tubes.

4. Wire the three loops together at several points underneath the blooms so that the wire is hidden.

## VIBURNUM
# RECIPE 4:
### CENTERPIECE

---

### INGREDIENTS

5 viburnum branches

2 stems of mock orange

2 peonies

6 parrot tulips

### MATERIALS

Large bowl

Flower frog

Floral putty

Place the flower frog in the bottom of the bowl and secure with floral putty.

2 Trim and add the viburnum branches, placing the shorter branches in the center and letting the longer branches trail out of the bowl to the right and left sides.

3 Trim the stems of mock orange, adding a long piece to the left alongside the viburnum, and a shorter piece to the right side of the arrangement. Trim and add the peonies in the center of the arrangement.

4 Finish by trimming and adding the parrot tulips to the bottom right side of the arrangement so that the blooms spill out of the bowl.

Highlight the reach of both viburnum branches and mock orange in an asymmetrical arrangement. The weight of the branches is balanced by tulips and hefty peonies.

SUMMER

# APPLE

What better way to welcome summer than by displaying a big juicy piece of it right in your home? Because of their obvious edible popularity, apple branches are somewhat rare at flower markets, but a branch abundant with fruit is worth tracking down. Two more butterfly favorites, buddleia and yarrow, help set the summery scene.

*apple*

*ivy*

*buddleia*

*yarrow*

APPLE

# RECIPE 1:
## PLACE SETTING

———

### INGREDIENTS

1 apple

1 leaf

**Create the perfect apple by adding on a leaf.**

1. Make a pinhole near the stem of the apple, insert the leaf into the hole so that it is secure, and place the apple at the center of a plate or napkin.

APPLE
# RECIPE 2:
WREATH

———

### INGREDIENTS
2 vines of ivy

### MATERIALS
Medium-gauge wire

**Thanks to its winding ways, a few vines of variegated ivy effortlessly coil into an elegant wreath.**

1.  Bend each vine of ivy into a round shape and wire the tip to the cut end.

2.  Lay one loop on top of the other and attach with wire in three places to secure.

APPLE
# RECIPE 3:
## CENTERPIECE

---

### INGREDIENTS

2 apple branches

6 vines of ivy

10 stems of yarrow

3 stems of buddleia

### MATERIALS

Large bowl

Large flower frog

Floral putty

**Vines of ivy stretch to new lengths, while fluffy bunches of buddleia and yarrow add to the garden feeling of this centerpiece.**

1. Place the flower frog in the bottom of the bowl and secure with floral putty. Trim and add the apple branches so that one extends to the right side of the bowl and one extends to the left.

2. Trim and add the ivy to the left so that the vines extend far out and cascade across the left side of the display surface.

3. Trim and add three stems of yarrow so that they arc at the top right and lower left of the arrangement. Trim and cluster the remaining seven stems of yarrow in the center around the apples.

4. Finish by trimming and adding one stem of buddleia to the left, and the remaining two stems to the right side to balance the trailing ivy.

# APPLE
# RECIPE 4:
## WREATH

---

### INGREDIENTS

1 apple branch

3 stems of buddleia

7 stems of yarrow

4 vines of ivy

### MATERIALS

Grapevine wreath frame

Heavy-gauge wire

3 water tubes

Small plastic bag

Wet paper towel

Rubber band

**Bring the best parts of the orchard in with a trimmed-down apple branch, heavy with fruit.**

1. Lay the apple branch diagonally across the center of the grapevine wreath frame and secure it with wire at the top and bottom. Trim the apple branch stem so that it does not extend beyond the frame.

2. Trim and tube the stems of buddleia and attach with heavy-gauge wire to the upper right side.

3. Gather the yarrow into a rounded cluster and bag (see page 18). Attach the bagged yarrow below the buddleia, covering the tubes.

4. Tuck in the ivy below the yarrow, taking care to conceal the bag with the leaves.

# BLACKBERRY

With its large green leaves, delicate white flowers, and red berries, blackberry branches are colorful and textural wonders at every stage. Fragrant lavender, feathery agonis, and dainty cosmos round out this laid-back bunch, all of which dry well. Because of their thorns, be sure to wear gardening gloves when handling blackberry branches.

*blackberry*

*cosmos*

*lavender*

*agonis*

BLACKBERRY

# RECIPE 1:
## GARLAND

————

### INGREDIENTS

9 blackberry branches

60 stems of lavender

6 stems of agonis

### MATERIALS

Rubber bands

Nine 12-inch pieces
of ribbon

Fishing line

**Not only is this garland lovely and fragrant, but if left suspended in place, it also will dry beautifully.**

1. Gather three blackberry branches, rubber band them together, and cover the rubber band by tying a piece of ribbon around the bunch. Repeat to create two more bunches.

2. Follow step 1 to make three bunches each of lavender and agonis.

3. Hang a thin piece of fishing line. Gently spread the stems of one bunch of lavender apart below the ribbon and nestle the bunch onto the fishing line so that the blooms face down. Proceed to hang the remaining bunches of lavender, agonis, and blackberry branches, alternating among the three different types.

BLACKBERRY
## RECIPE 2:
### FOCAL ARRANGEMENT

---

#### INGREDIENTS
4 blackberry branches

16 stems of lavender

1 stem of agonis

9 cosmos

#### MATERIALS
Small vase

**Leave the stems of this dark and fruity arrangement extra long to create dramatic arches and curves.**

1. Trim and add three blackberry branches to the right side of the vase, and one branch to the left side.

2. Divide the lavender into two clusters and trim and add one to the right side and one to the left side of the arrangement.

3. Trim and add the stem of agonis to the left side of the arrangement.

4. Finish by adding the stems of cosmos, trimmed to varying heights throughout the arrangement, placing the longer stems to the right to balance the agonis on the left.

BLACKBERRY
# RECIPE 3:
WREATH

———

## INGREDIENTS

30 sprigs of blackberry

## MATERIALS

Honeysuckle wreath
frame

Paddle wire

Start with the honeysuckle
wreath frame.

Trim the leaves from the blackberry
sprigs and reserve them for use later.
Gather two sprigs of blackberry and lay
them on top of the frame. Wrap paddle
wire around the stems and frame several
times to secure them in place.

3  Continue adding and wiring the sprigs
to the frame so that each new bundle
covers the exposed stems of the
previous one, and proceed around
the entire frame.

4  When it's time to add the final bundle,
tuck the stems underneath the berries
of the first cluster and wire to the frame.
Finish by adding the reserved foliage,
tucking the leaves in at various points
throughout the wreath.

Use branches with berries at various stages of ripeness to fully appreciate the blackberry's palette.

*cotoneaster*

*purple sage*

*pomegranate*

# COTONEASTER

Cotoneaster might be a victim of its own success. Because it's considered an invasive weed in some parts of the country (due to its effortless growth), you may have overlooked this ubiquitous evergreen in the past. Sturdy but bendable branches covered with little leafy greens make a great foundation for wreaths and garlands. Cotoneaster berries appear in reds and oranges, but branches with unripe berries add plenty of visual interest. Strawflower, fragrant purple sage, and pomegranate come together in a muted but colorful palette, all of which will dry well.

*strawflower*

*pomegranate*

COTONEASTER
## RECIPE 1:
WREATH

———

**INGREDIENTS**
22 strawflowers

**MATERIALS**
Heavy-gauge wire

**String together a collection of strawflowers to create a color-wheel effect.**

1.  Cut two lengths of heavy-gauge wire.

2.  Trim the heads off the strawflowers and thread them onto the first wire, graduating the colors slightly as you continue around the circle.

3.  When you have achieved the desired color blend, gently bend the wire into a circle.

4.  Twist the ends of the wire together at the back of the wreath to close the loop.

5.  Repeat for the second wreath.

## COTONEASTER
# RECIPE 2:
## PLACE SETTING

---

### INGREDIENTS
2 pomegranates

### MATERIALS
2 birch slices

Heavy-gauge wire

**A matrix of pomegranate seeds is revealed to guests with a simple slice.**

1. Cut two short pieces of heavy-gauge wire and hammer them into the birch slices.

2. Cut a pomegranate in half to reveal the seeds and slide the halves onto the wires at interesting angles.

3. Arrange the log slices and the second pomegranate into a pleasing composition.

COTONEASTER
## RECIPE 3:
WREATH

———

### INGREDIENTS
2 branches of
cotoneaster

16 strawflowers

5 stems of sage

### MATERIALS
Wire wreath frame

Thin-gauge wire

**Cotoneaster appears to be holding itself in a perfect circle thanks to the work of a hidden frame and the branch's own wild and weedy disposition.**

1. Bend the branches of cotoneaster around the wire wreath frame and secure with thin-gauge wire.

2. Gather eleven strawflowers and three stems of sage and attach with wire to the bottom of the frame.

3. Gather the remaining ingredients. Lay the bundle next to the first one, facing in the opposite direction. Tuck the stems under the blooms of the first bundle to conceal them and attach with wire.

### INGREDIENTS

3 branches of
cotoneaster

8 pomegranates,
on the branch
or skewered

8 stems of purple sage

16 strawflowers

### MATERIALS

Twine

Paddle wire

Cut twine to the desired
length of your garland. Using
the sectional cutting method
(see page 11), trim the
cotoneaster branches into
sprigs that are 4 to 6 inches
long.

2 Gather a sprig of cotoneaster and two
pomegranates and attach them to the
twine with paddle wire.

3 Gather a stem of sage and two
strawflowers and attach them to the
twine with paddle wire.

4 Continue to gather ingredients, working
your way down the twine and securing
each bundle with paddle wire. Secure the
last bundle to the twine in the opposite
direction.

This bountiful garland is filled with fragrance and texture and will dry beautifully. It'll likely be too heavy to hang, but drapes attractively along the length of a table.

*eucalyptus*

*yarrow*

# EUCALYPTUS

One waft of fresh eucalyptus transports us to the wild shores of Australia. Different varieties produce unique seedpods and flowers almost alien in their beauty. Its leaves come in shades of pale green and silver that fade into orange, red, and brown when dried, and its invigorating fragrance is unrivaled. Pairing eucalyptus with kangaroo paw references its origins, and yarrow and caspia are right at home with this desert-loving bunch.

*kangaroo paw*

*eucalyptus*

*caspia*

# RECIPE 1:
## PLACE SETTING

———

### INGREDIENTS

1 branch of eucalyptus

1 sprig of
kangaroo paw

1 stem of yarrow

### MATERIALS

Medium-gauge wire

With subtle silver tones, a long twist of eucalyptus acts as a tiny wreath as it holds on to a guest's napkin.

1. Loop the eucalyptus branch around itself and secure with medium-gauge wire.

2. Tuck the kangaroo paw and yarrow through the eucalyptus.

### INGREDIENTS

6 branches of
eucalyptus, assorted
varieties and sizes

4 branches of
kangaroo paw

6 stems of caspia

### MATERIALS

Branch

Medium-gauge wire

**A vertical branch garland on your front door is a nice alternative to a traditional round wreath.**

1.  Divide the ingredients into three similar bundles, reserving a stem of eucalyptus.

2.  Hold the first bundle in place on the branch and secure with medium-gauge wire. Attach the second bundle on top of the first, covering its stems.

3.  Attach the last bundle to the branch in the opposite direction. Tuck in the reserved eucalyptus to conceal any exposed stems and wire.

---

### INGREDIENTS

6 branches of
eucalyptus

6 stems of
kangaroo paw

6 stems of seeded
eucalyptus

6 stems of caspia

4 stems of yarrow

### MATERIALS

Double-ring wreath
frame

Paddle wire

**1** Create a bundle from a variety of the ingredients and lay it on top of the double-ring wreath frame. Wrap paddle wire around the stems and the frame several times to secure them in place.

**2** Continue making bundles and wiring them to the frame so that each new bundle covers the exposed stems of the previous one.

**3** As you work your way around the wreath, tuck in longer pieces of eucalyptus as needed to make the wreath balanced.

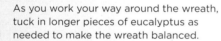

**4** Finish by tucking the stems of the last bundle beneath the first.

Showcase every unique facet of the eucalyptus branch—fragrance, flower, seed, and all—in a massive and overreaching wreath.

# HUCKLEBERRY

Huckleberry is a wild branch that doesn't care to be cultivated, preferring to live in forests and along hillsides. Its hardy green branches provide a strong visual foundation for arrangements, while delicate, sweet elements such as honeysuckle and chamomile soften the grouping. Expect branches to last 2 to 3 weeks in water.

*honeysuckle*

*ornamental grass*

*globe clover*

*huckleberry*

*chamomile*

# RECIPE 1:
## PLACE SETTING

———

### INGREDIENTS

4 huckleberry sprigs

4 vines of honeysuckle

10 stems of
globe clover

3 stems of chamomile

8 stems of ornamental
grass

### MATERIALS

4 feathers

Five 8-inch pieces
of ribbon

Floral tape

**Bits of flowers, feathers, and twigs come together in one-of-a-kind collections. Use as place settings or boutonnieres for casual events.**

1. Gather a random variety of the listed ingredients to create five unique bundles.

2. Secure each by wrapping with floral tape just below the blooms.

3. Tie on a ribbon, making sure to cover the floral tape.

4. Trim the stems to 2 inches below the ribbon.

---

### INGREDIENTS

15 sprigs of chamomile

12 stems of
globe clover

### MATERIALS

Bind wire

1 yard of ribbon

Paddle wire

**Reminiscent of a daisy chain, this petite swag could be worn as a necklace.**

1. Cut a piece of bind wire to the desired length of your swag.

2. Gather several sprigs of chamomile and globe clover. Hold the bundle onto one end of the bind wire and secure with paddle wire.

3. Gather a second bundle and lay it on top of the first to conceal the stems. Secure in place with paddle wire. Repeat the process with three more bundles.

4. Finish by securing the last bundle to the bind wire in the opposite direction. Attach the ribbon to the back of the garland and hang.

### INGREDIENTS

2 huckleberry branches

2 stems of chamomile

8 stems of
ornamental grass

5 honeysuckle vines

### MATERIALS

Tall, narrow vase

9 feathers

9 pieces of extra-thin-
gauge wire, cut to
5- to 8-inch lengths

**Suspended feathers appear to be floating among the branches of huckleberry, adding movement and levity to this airy arrangement.**

1. Trim and add a long branch of huckleberry to the left side of the vase so that it arcs outward, and trim and add the other branch leaning out on the right side.

2. Trim and add the stems of chamomile to the upper left side of the vase, above the huckleberry.

3. Trim and add the stems of ornamental grass to the center right side, and a honeysuckle vine on each side of the composition. Trim and add the remaining three stems of honeysuckle front and center at the rim.

4. Wrap a piece of thin-gauge wire around the end of a feather, attaching the other end of the wire to the left side of the huckleberry branch. Continue wrapping feathers with wire and attaching them along the length of the huckleberry branch, at varying heights. Finish by adding a few to the right side.

### INGREDIENTS

2 huckleberry branches

### MATERIALS

Thin-gauge wire

3 feathers, wired

Start with two long, flexible huckleberry branches.

2 Bend each branch into a round shape, wiring the tip to the end so you have two loops. Nestle the loops together, then secure with wire. Finish by attaching the feathers to the bottom of the wreath.

Huckleberry's malleable properties come in handy when creating a wild, nest-like wreath.

# KANGAROO PAW

Furry and finger-like, the small blooms of kangaroo paw pack a powerful punch of color. Alongside a geometrical succulent and tufts of hydrangea, they create an unrivaled textural palette. Kangaroo paw flowers will last for several weeks if the stems are recut and the water is changed regularly, and they will dry nicely when hung upside down.

*rudbeckia*

*sedum*

*succulent*

*kangaroo paw*

*hydrangea*

*succulent*

# RECIPE 1:
## PLACE SETTING

———

### INGREDIENTS

5 succulent heads

### MATERIALS

Five 4-inch pieces
of ribbon

Floral glue

**Nature has done most of the work with this play on a prize ribbon.**

1. Cut a V-tongue shape into one end of a piece of ribbon.

2. Using a dot of floral glue, attach the ribbon to the underside of the succulent head. Place faceup.

3. Repeat with the remaining succulents.

# RECIPE 2:
## CENTERPIECE

———

### INGREDIENTS

3 stems of hydrangea

3 stems of sedum

3 kangaroo paw
branches

5 stems of rudbeckia

### MATERIALS

Creamer

**Button-faced rudbeckia shine in this sunny arrangement.**

1. Trim and add the stems of hydrangea and sedum to the creamer to build the base of the arrangement.

2. Trim and add the branches of kangaroo paw in a cluster to the right side of the creamer.

3. Finish by trimming and adding the stems of rudbeckia: three stems to the center front and two longer stems to the far left to balance the kangaroo paw.

## KANGAROO PAW
# RECIPE 3:
### WREATH

---

#### INGREDIENTS

7 kangaroo paw
branches

3 wired succulents

3 stems of sedum

3 stems of hydrangea

#### MATERIALS

Grapevine wreath
frame

3 water tubes

Medium-gauge wire

Start with the grapevine
wreath frame.

2 Tuck in five branches of kangaroo paw
to the bottom of the frame and secure in
place with medium-gauge wire.

3 Add a wired succulent, a tubed
hydrangea, and a stem of sedum,
wiring the ingredients onto the
frame so that they cover the stems
of the kangaroo paw.

4 Continue attaching the remaining
ingredients until you have gone three
quarters of the way around the frame,
making sure to conceal the hydrangea
tubes. Finish by tucking two shorter
branches of kangaroo paw into the
wreath on the right side.

To make a long-lasting version of this wreath, replace the hydrangea with extra succulents and sedum.

# LEUCADENDRON

The small cone-like florets that line leucadendron branches mimic their larger king protea cousins, albeit on a much smaller scale. Hanging amaranthus adds velvety texture, while freesia brings a pop of fresh color and fragrance to a rich and complex gathering. Many different varieties of leucadendron can last several days out of water and dry beautifully.

*king protea*

*leucadendron*

*freesia*

*amaranthus*

LEUCADENDRON
# RECIPE 1:
## PLACE SETTING

————

**INGREDIENTS**

2 stems of freesia

**MATERIALS**

2 birch slices

Heavy-gauge wire

Use the natural curve of the freesia to create an interestingly angled place setting or add more pieces down the length of a table for a sprouting centerpiece. Freesia can survive well out of water for a day.

1. Cut two short pieces of heavy-gauge wire and hammer them into the birch slices.

2. Trim a stem of freesia to the desired length and slide it onto the wire through the center of the stem. Repeat with the second birch slice and stem of freesia.

# RECIPE 2:
## FOCAL ARRANGEMENT

---

### INGREDIENTS

6 leucadendron branches

2 stems of amaranthus

4 stems of freesia

### MATERIALS

Medium bowl

Flower frog

Floral putty

**The simple rustic style of this arrangement is easily achieved by clustering textural ingredients.**

1. Place the flower frog in the bottom of the bowl and secure with floral putty. Cut three long branches of leucadendron and add them to the back so that they extend above the rest of the arrangement.

2. Trim the remaining three branches of leucadendron to shorter lengths and fill in the center of the arrangement.

3. Trim and add the amaranthus to the left side so that it rests on the rim of the bowl and spills out onto the display surface.

4. Finish by trimming and adding three stems of freesia clustered on the front right side, and trimming and adding one stem of freesia high on the right to balance the tall leucadendron.

# RECIPE 3:
## WALL HANGING

---

### INGREDIENTS

5 leucadendron
branches, yielding
125 florets

### MATERIALS

Six 1-yard pieces
of ribbon

Floral glue

Birch branch

1 yard of burlap ribbon

**Inspired by lengths of embroidered Swiss ribbon, this piece will dry nicely, creating a reusable wall hanging.**

1. Snip the florets off the leucadendron branches, leaving some foliage at the base of each floret.

2. Take one piece of ribbon and dot it with floral glue, then attach a floret. Continue, adding dots of glue and florets about 1 inch apart and facing the same direction along the length of ribbon until you have attached twenty-five florets. Repeat this step four more times with the remaining ribbons and florets.

3. Once the glue has dried, tie each ribbon to the birch branch. Attach the burlap ribbon to each end of the birch branch for hanging.

## LEUCADENDRON
# RECIPE 4:
### SWAG

————

### INGREDIENTS

8 leucadendron
branches

2 stems of king protea

2 stems of hanging
amaranthus

4 stems of freesia

### MATERIALS

2 yards of ribbon

Trim the leucadendron branches to a similar length and lay them on your work surface.

 Trim the stems of king protea and add them on top of the leucadendron so that the heads lie in the middle of the branches when the stems are aligned.

3 Trim the stems of amaranthus and add them on top of the grouping so that the heads lie just below the king protea.

4 Tie the grouping with the ribbon, trimming the ends as necessary. Fan out the leucadendron slightly in the back and hang the swag. Finish by tucking in the stems of freesia: one on the left and three on the right.

The king protea takes center stage in this swag, but the weight of its supporting cast keeps everything in balance, visually and structurally.

*pokeberry*

*dahlia*

# POKEBERRY

Pokeberry's bright pink stems and black berries are often used as natural dyes. Grasses, vines, and pods blend well with the wild berries in a summertime textural explosion. All parts of the pokeberry plant are toxic when eaten, so take extra care to keep it away from pets and infants.

*ornamental grass*

*jasmine*

*echinacea pods*

---

### INGREDIENTS

1 sprig of pokeberry branch

2 echinacea pods

1 stem of ornamental grass

### MATERIALS

Floral tape

10-inch piece of ribbon

**A small posy or boutonniere wrapped in a country ribbon draws attention to a bare echinacea pod and tiny rows of pokeberry.**

1. Gather the pokeberry, echinacea, and ornamental grass.

2. Secure by wrapping with floral tape just below the blooms.

3. Tie on the ribbon, making sure to cover the floral tape.

4. Trim the stems to 2 inches below the ribbon.

POKEBERRY

# RECIPE 2:
## WREATH

————

### INGREDIENTS

4 vines of jasmine

### MATERIALS

2 wire frames

Thin-gauge wire

**Despite having such small flowers, jasmine gives off a powerful fragrance; a thin and simple wreath will easily fill the rooms of your home with a sweet scent.**

1. Curve two vines of jasmine around a wire frame and secure it with thin-gauge wire.

2. Attach the remaining jasmine vines around the second frame, clustering them on the upper left side, leaving some of the frame exposed.

1 | Start with the honeysuckle wreath frame.

2 Gather three sprigs of pokeberry and use paddle wire to attach the bundle to the bottom of the frame. Gather four more sprigs of pokeberry and attach them on top of the first bundle.

3 Tuck the stems of ornamental grass in just above the pokeberry. Attach the echinacea pods in a cluster along the upper right side of the wreath.

4 Finish by tucking the jasmine vines and the remaining three pokeberry sprigs around the wreath.

A spray of unripe pokeberries brings a pop of electric green to a viney wreath.

# POKEBERRY
# RECIPE 4:
## CENTERPIECE

___

### INGREDIENTS

10 branches of
pokeberry

5 vines of jasmine

20 dahlias

8 stems of
ornamental grass

### MATERIALS

2 rectangular
papier-mâché pots

6 flower frogs

Floral putty

Place the flower frogs in
the bottoms of the pots
and secure with floral putty.

2  Trim and add the branches of pokeberry
to the pots so that they create a full,
dense base.

3  Trim and add the vines of jasmine
throughout the arrangement so that
they extend outward just beyond the
pokeberry.

4  Trim and add the dahlias throughout
the center of the arrangement at varying
heights. Finish by trimming and adding
the stems of ornamental grass.

This sprawling arrangement is easily created when two low containers are nestled side by side.

# AUTUMN

# BITTERSWEET

Although bittersweet is considered a nuisance (and is illegal to sell) in some parts of the country, often killing trees and other plants in its wake, it's impossible to hate it outright. All along bittersweet's rambling vines, beautiful yellow pods crack open to reveal bright red berries. Its longevity as a cut branch makes it appealing for out-of-water arrangements. Paired with marigolds, safflowers, and chrysanthemums, it creates a powerful autumn palette.

*marigold*

*safflower*

bittersweet

chrysanthemum

## BITTERSWEET
# RECIPE 1:
## CENTERPIECE

### INGREDIENTS

48 marigolds

22 stems of safflower

48 chrysanthemums

3 bittersweet branches

**This site-built mandala uses a repeating pattern and radial symmetry to create a full yet simple centerpiece.**

1. Trim the heads off of all the marigolds, safflowers, and chrysanthemums.

2. Working directly on your display surface, start with a small circle of marigold heads in the center, and continue to build around the circle concentrically with the other marigold heads, safflowers, bittersweet branches, and chrysanthemum heads. Use the photograph as a guide, if desired. Cut the bittersweet branches down to size as needed.

## INGREDIENTS

1 bittersweet branch

24 small marigolds

24 large marigolds

## MATERIALS

Embroidery needle

Fishing line

1 yard of cord

A berry-filled branch of bittersweet can hold a mass of marigolds, both large and small, and those eye-catching berries save it from fading into the background.

1.  Trim the heads off the large marigolds and string sixteen heads on a piece of fishing line using the embroidery needle. Attach one end of the fishing line at the right side of the bittersweet branch, and the other end of the line to the left side. Pull up the center of the marigold garland and loop it on a twig of the bittersweet to create a *W* shape.

2.  String the rest of the large marigold heads on another piece of fishing line and attach one end of the line on the right side of the branch, and the other end to the center of the first marigold garland so that it hangs below the first garland.

3.  Trim the heads off the small marigolds and string onto a piece of fishing line, attaching one end to the right side of the bittersweet branch and the other end to the left side so that it hangs below the other garlands.

4.  Attach the cord to each end of the bittersweet branch for hanging.

1 | Start with the grapevine wreath frame.

2 | Place five bittersweet branches at the top of the frame so that they follow the curve but are still wild and unruly. Wire the branches in place to secure them.

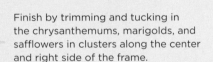

3 | Continue adding the remaining three bittersweet branches, securing them in place.

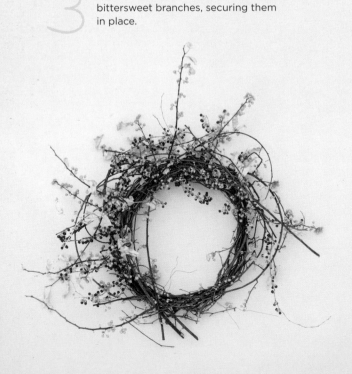

4 | Finish by trimming and tucking in the chrysanthemums, marigolds, and safflowers in clusters along the center and right side of the frame.

Instead of trying to tame bittersweet, use its wildness to your advantage by highlighting tangles.

*hawthorn*

# HAWTHORN

Although its sweet white-and-pink blossoms and multihued berries won't go unnoticed, it's hawthorn's saw-toothed leaves that make this branch a year-round winner. Petite gourds with unruly stems and feathery pistachio leaves add some playfulness to the mix. Hawthorn by all means lives up to its name: use caution when handling this spiny branch.

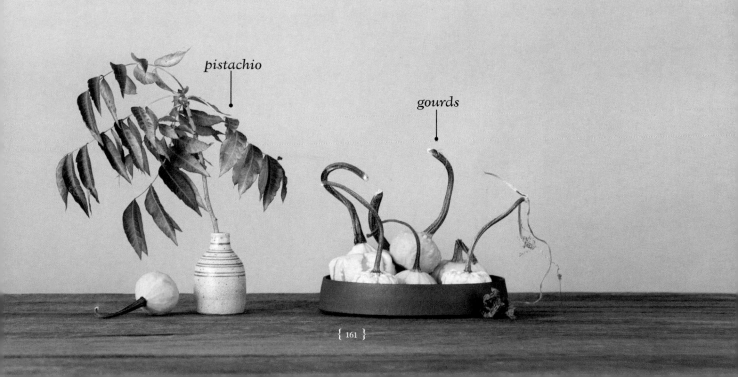

*pistachio*

*gourds*

### INGREDIENTS
2 gourds

4 hawthorn leaves

2 clusters of
hawthorn berry

1 twig of pistachio
with leaves

### MATERIALS
Large platter

**Let each ingredient speak for itself in a simple, specimen-style display.**

1. Assemble a collection of the ingredients on the platter, spacing them far enough apart so that each element can be seen and enjoyed.

# RECIPE 2:
## GARLAND

---

### INGREDIENTS

9 gourds of various
colors and shapes

### MATERIALS

Long heavy-gauge
needle

Heavy-gauge
fishing line

Hammer

Nails

Six 1-yard-long
pieces of ribbon

**Get your gourds off the ground and present them in a new light as a garland.**

1. Drive the heavy-gauge needle threaded with heavy-duty fishing line through the gourds, using a hammer to tap it through if there is too much resistance. Leave 6 inches of fishing line at each end.

2. Attach the garland to the wall using nails, and tie three pieces of ribbon to each end of the garland to conceal any exposed fishing line.

HAWTHORN
# RECIPE 3:
## WREATH

———

### INGREDIENTS

3 hawthorn branches

4 sprigs of pistachio

3 gourds, skewered
(see page 17)

### MATERIALS

Grapevine wreath
frame

Medium-gauge wire

1 Layer two hawthorn branches on top of each other and bend them around the right half of the grapevine wreath frame; secure in place with medium-gauge wire.

2 Lay the last hawthorn branch around the left side of the wreath. Secure the branch with wire.

3 Trim the ends of the branches that hang over the edge of the wreath. Then tuck two sprigs of pistachio into the bottom-left side of the wreath.

4 Tuck the skewered gourds into the bottom of the wreath, on top of the pistachio. Finish by adding the remaining two sprigs of pistachio into the left and right sides of the wreath.

If your hawthorn branch has too many leaves, remove some to reveal the clusters of berries.

# LIQUIDAMBAR

We can't think of another tree whose name first conjures images of rare, fiery gemstones instead of its actual botanical self. Named for its fragrant, resin-like sap, it also lives up to its name when you see the golden amber tones of its autumn foliage. Look for branches that still have their star-like seedpod attached for added interest. This bright collection of ingredients performs well out of water.

*rose hips*

*callicarpa berry*

*aster*

*liquidambar*

# LIQUIDAMBAR
# RECIPE 1:
## WALL HANGING

————

### INGREDIENTS
1 liquidambar branch

### MATERIALS
4 colors of embroidery floss

**The shape of the branch and the colorful thread of this swag will keep things interesting even after the leaves have fallen.**

1.  Wrap the branch of liquidambar in embroidery floss at different points across the branch, varying the color combinations and widths of the wrappings.

2.  When finished wrapping, let the ends of the threads hang long and loose below the branch.

# RECIPE 2:
## GARLAND

———

### INGREDIENTS

16 liquidambar leaves

11 asters

55 rose hips

6 sprigs of
callicarpa berries

### MATERIALS

Embroidery needle

Six 1-yard-long pieces
of fishing line

**Leaves, berries, flowers, and fruits become botanical wallpaper when strung on an invisible line.**

1.  Using the embroidery needle, thread five liquidambar leaves onto the first piece of fishing line. Then thread the second line with the asters; the third line with the rose hips; the fourth line with six liquidambar leaves; the fifth line with the sprigs of callicarpa berries; and the sixth line with the remaining five liquidambar leaves.

2.  Hang each piece of fishing line on a wall several inches apart.

Start with the wire wreath frame. Gather a variety of the listed ingredients to create a small bundle.

 Attach the bundle to the frame with paddle wire. Gather a second bundle and attach it on top of the first with paddle wire.

3 Continue making and attaching bundles, slightly varying the number of each ingredient. Trim any stems that extend too far off the frame.

4 Tuck the stems of the final bundle under the first bundle.

Star-shaped leaves and bright berries form a
petite ring of autumnal fireworks.

# MAGNOLIA

The thick, leathery leaves of the magnolia tree are glossy green on top, but we're more interested in their velvety brown underside. Magnolia leaves are hardy and look as good dried in a garland as they do plucked from the tree, but its large, fragrant flowers bruise easily and tend to drop their petals quickly. Spiny artichokes, sunflowers, and shaggy grasses add interesting texture to the group.

*magnolia*

*sunflower*

*artichoke*

*ornamental grass*

---

### INGREDIENTS

30 magnolia leaves

### MATERIALS

Wire wreath frame

Thin-gauge wire

1 yard of ribbon

**Challenge the notion that every wreath needs greenery by using the underside of magnolia leaves to create an uncomplicated ring.**

1. Using thin-gauge wire, attach the stem of a magnolia leaf, green side down, to the wire wreath frame.

2. Continue to wire on the magnolia leaves, making sure that each new leaf covers the stem of the previous leaf.

3. Attach the ribbon at two points on the back of the frame and hang.

### INGREDIENTS

1 magnolia branch

5 artichokes
with stems

2 sunflowers

7 stems of
ornamental grass

### MATERIALS

1 yard of ribbon

Floral tape

**Sunflowers, artichokes, and wheat-like grass are harvested together and unified with a few large, smooth magnolia leaves.**

1. Gather the magnolia branch and two long stems of artichoke.

2. Add two sunflowers to the bunch so that the heads lean to the left. Then add six stems of ornamental grass to the right, and one stem of ornamental grass to the left.

3. Add the remaining three artichoke stems low in the front. Secure the bunch with floral tape, and tie a bow with ribbon, concealing the floral tape. Finish by trimming all the stems to five inches below the ribbon.

## MAGNOLIA
# RECIPE 3:
## GARLAND

——————

### INGREDIENTS

4 sunflowers

4 artichokes

15 stems of
ornamental grass

3 magnolia leaves

### MATERIALS

Embroidery floss

Embroidery needle

**A long line of flowers, leaves, and grasses tumbles down the wall in the rusty tones of autumn.**

1. Trim the heads from the sunflowers and artichokes. Divide the ornamental grass into three bundles and tie them together with a short piece of embroidery floss.

2. Using the embroidery needle, thread embroidery floss through the elements in a random order.

3. Alternate the directions of the magnolia leaves and grass posies as you go, until you've reached the desired length.

*maple*

*oak*

# MAPLE

With its broad, multipoint leaves that turn spectacular shades of red, it's no wonder the maple leaf became the icon for an entire country. Over the course of a year, maple trees run the gamut in the color department— from dark green in spring and summer to yellow-orange in early autumn and, finally, trademark red by the time the season is wrapping up. Rather than add flowers to the mix, pair maple with similarly interesting leaves and embrace what autumn is all about.

*dogwood*

*maple*

MAPLE

# RECIPE 1:
## PLACE SETTING

———

### INGREDIENTS
6 leaves of
different sizes

### MATERIALS
Embroidery needle

Embroidery floss

**Although we appreciate the beauty of a large maple tree bursting with color, the elegant silhouette of the leaves on their own is just as impactful.**

1. Using the largest leaf as your base, layer a slightly smaller leaf on top of it, and the smallest leaf on top of that.

2. Use a needle threaded with embroidery floss to stitch an X in the center of all three leaves to secure them together. Tie a knot on the back to secure. Repeat with the remaining three leaves.

### INGREDIENTS

13 leaves of various
sizes and colors

3 twigs

### MATERIALS

2 large branches
or sticks

1 yard of leather cord

Thin-gauge thread

Leaves suspended in midair bring autumn indoors in a most literal way. Use whatever leaves and twigs you have on hand to make this easy mobile.

1.  Place the branches across each other in an *X* and bind them together using the leather cord, leaving at least 12 inches for hanging.

2.  Tie a piece of thread around each leaf and twig and attach at varying lengths along the branches.

MAPLE
# RECIPE 3:
WREATH

—

### INGREDIENTS
6 dogwood branches

6 maple branches

6 oak branches

### MATERIALS
Wire wreath frame

Paddle wire

1 Secure a branch of dogwood to the right side of the wire wreath frame with paddle wire.

2 Trim one dogwood branch, one maple branch, and one oak branch into smaller pieces and assemble small bundles with a mix of the elements. Secure a bundle on the right side of the frame with paddle wire just below the first branch of dogwood.

3 Continue working clockwise around the frame, alternating between adding small bundles and single larger branches.

4 Finish by adding the final bundle to the top of the frame.

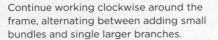

Go all out with a wreath comprised of all of autumn's favorite leaves and colors.

# PERSIMMON

The combination of orchids and persimmons lends an unexpected and slightly exotic touch to this autumnal collection. The most common types of persimmons are the Hachiya and the Fuyu, but although both varieties turn an intense orange when fully ripe, they have distinctively different profiles. Hachiya are more oblong and somewhat heart-shaped, while Fuyu are squat and round like a tomato. Both varieties are used in the recipes here, but no matter which you use, make sure that the fruit is still hard and not yet ripe; no one wants a squishy persimmon falling off the wall!

*persimmon*

orchid

ornamental grass

dried hydrangea

# RECIPE 1:
## CENTERPIECE

————

**INGREDIENTS**

5 persimmons

**MATERIALS**

Medium bowl

**Less-ripe persimmons going through their color changes create a perfect palette for transitioning from summer to autumn.**

1. Trim five persimmon fruits so that short stems are still intact, and arrange them in the bowl.

———

### INGREDIENTS

4 persimmon branches

3 stems of dried hydrangea

3 stems of orchids

### MATERIALS

Medium vase

Flower frog

Floral putty

**Angular persimmon branches, heavy with fruit, contrast nicely with an arc of orchids in this lacy arrangement.**

1. Place the flower frog in the bottom of the vase and secure with floral putty. Trim and add the persimmon branches to the vase so that the weight is evenly balanced.

2. Add the stems of hydrangea to the middle and left side to fill in between the fruit.

3. Finish by adding one stem of orchid to the lower front of the arrangement, and the remaining two stems of orchids to the right side.

---

### INGREDIENTS

3 persimmon branches

5 stems of
dried hydrangea

4 stems of orchids

7 stems of
ornamental grass

### MATERIALS

Honeysuckle wreath
frame

Medium-gauge wire

**1** Start with the honeysuckle wreath frame.

**2** Use medium-gauge wire to attach the persimmon branches to the bottom left side of the frame.

**3** Tuck one stem of hydrangea into the frame at the bottom between the persimmons, and tuck in the remaining four stems of hydrangea up along the right side of the frame.

**4** Tuck in three stems of orchids between the stems of hydrangea on the right side, trimming any stems that extend beyond the frame. Add the last orchid to the bottom center, and finish by tucking in the ornamental grass around the right side of the wreath.

If you fail to find an abundantly filled persimmon branch for this recipe, no worries: wiring the fruit isn't cheating and it's just as lovely.

# PLUM

It's the leaves of the plum tree—the cherry plum to be specific—that really make it stand out amid a sea of verdant and fruitful branches. A close relative of cherry, the plum has large, pink blossoms and rusty foliage in spring; later in the season, the leaves and branches turn a beautiful purple-black color. The dusty pinks of astilbe and blushing bride protea take on a decidedly more mature character when paired with plum.

*astilbe*

*scabiosa*

*plum*

*protea*

### INGREDIENTS

3 plum branches

6 stems of astilbe

3 stems of protea

4 stems of scabiosa

### MATERIALS

Gold spray paint

Medium vase

**Add some easy sparkle to a centerpiece with a few stripped-down branches painted gold.**

1. Remove all of the leaves from two plum branches and spray them with the spray paint. Allow to dry.

2. Trim and add a short plum branch to the right side of the vase, and trim and add the stems of astilbe to fill out the center and left side of the arrangement. Add the painted branches to the back of the vase.

3. Trim and add the stems of blushing bride protea to the front of the arrangement, clustering them low and in the center.

4. Finish by trimming and adding three stems of scabiosa to the center of the arrangement, and one long stem of scabiosa so that it arcs out on the left side.

### INGREDIENTS

4 plum branches

2 stems of astilbe

2 stems of protea

### MATERIALS

4 yards of cord

Medium-gauge wire

An angular wreath can hang on its own or become a unique frame when a photograph is placed at the center, bringing special attention to guests of honor.

1. Lay the plum branches out in a square so that the ends overlap slightly. Secure them with medium-gauge wire at the four corners. Remove any excess foliage to define the shape of the frame.

2. Gather the stems of astilbe and blushing bride protea into two bundles.

3. Tie one bundle to the top of the plum branch frame with the cord so that the blooms are pointing to the right, and tie the other bundle to the bottom of the frame so that it faces in the opposite direction. Leave the ends of the cord long so that they hang down beyond the frame.

**INGREDIENTS**

1 plum branch

**MATERIALS**

Silver spray paint

Bronze spray paint

Gold spray paint

1 yard of rope

**The plum branch's deep, rich tone makes it the perfect canvas for a trio of metallics.**

1. Lay the plum branch on a flat work surface and, using spray paint, spray the bottom of the branch with silver, the lower midsection with bronze, and the upper midsection with gold.

2. Once the paint has completely dried, tie the rope to the branch, allowing the ends to hang down.

# PRIVET

If only all weeds could be as lovely as privet. Sure, it invades gardens and its flowers are unremarkable, but oh, the berries. A member of the olive family, privet practically bursts with tiny, purple-gray inedible berries that bring a rare shade and depth to arrangements and wreaths. The rich jewel tones found in heather, nandina, and in the dark centers of ornamental kale really make the little gems of privet shine.

*nandina*

*heather*

*ornamental kale*

*privet*

### INGREDIENTS

5 heads of
ornamental kale

10 sprigs of privet

5 stems of heather

5 stems of nandina

### MATERIALS

Large, shallow bowl

Chicken wire, cut to
fit the bowl

Waterproof tape

**The deep purples and pinks of privet, ornamental kale, and heather work together to create a colorful cornucopia.**

1. Form a rounded shape with the chicken wire and tape it in place in the bowl.

2. Insert the stems of kale through the chicken wire so that the heads of kale rest on top of the wire; three at the back left and two in the front center.

3. Trim and add the sprigs of privet to the middle and right front side of the arrangement at the rim of the bowl so that the berries hang low and touch the surface of the table.

4. Trim and add two stems of heather to the left side, and three on the right side. Finish by adding two stems of nandina to the back left of the arrangement and the remaining three stems of nandina to the back right.

PRIVET
# RECIPE 2:
WREATH

---

### INGREDIENTS
36 sprigs of privet

### MATERIALS
Wire wreath frame

Paddle wire

2 yards of ribbon, cut
into 1-yard-long pieces

**There's nothing remarkable about a single privet fruit on its own, but add a few hundred and now we're talking.**

1. Gather three sprigs of privet and attach them to the top of the wire wreath frame with paddle wire.

2. Continue adding and wiring the bundles of privet to the wreath so that each new bundle covers the exposed stems of the previous one, and proceed around the entire frame.

3. When it's time to add the final bundle, tuck the stems underneath the heads of the first cluster and wire it to the frame, making sure to conceal any exposed wire.

4. Finish by tying the ribbons to the lower left side of the wreath.

PRIVET
# RECIPE 3:
SWAG

———————

### INGREDIENTS

3 stems of nandina

5 sprigs of privet

3 stems of heather

### MATERIALS

Large branch

Paddle wire

2 yards of ribbon

1 | Start with the large branch.

2 | Gather a stem of nandina, a sprig of privet, and a stem of heather. Use paddle wire to attach the bundle to the branch.

3 | Gather a similar bundle and place it on top of the first so that it conceals the wiring and stems. Secure it with paddle wire.

4 | Gather the last bundle and attach it to the branch in the opposite direction. Finish by tucking in the final two sprigs of privet to conceal any visible wiring; then attach the ribbon to each end of the branch for hanging.

You may need to adjust the ribbon location or trim and turn the swag to find the best way to hang it against the wall.

# ROSEMARY

Evergreen rosemary suits every season, with its hardiness and strong fragrance. Commonly known as a symbol of remembrance, a sprig can give special meaning to arrangements. Grouping rosemary, delphinium, and asclepias eschews the common autumn color themes, and a few well-chosen pears create a farm-fresh palette that makes mouths water.

*delphinium*

*asclepias*

*rosemary*

*pear*

### INGREDIENTS

15 pears, hard and
not yet ripe

### MATERIALS

Long heavy-gauge
needle

Heavy-gauge
fishing line

Nails

2 yards of ribbon, cut
into 1-yard-long pieces

The mottled skins of petite pears create a bountiful garland. Be sure to use strong nails to mount this chunky piece.

1. Using the heavy-gauge needle threaded with heavy-gauge fishing line, string the pears, alternating the colors and orientation. Leave 6 inches of fishing line at each end for hanging.

2. Attach the garland to the wall using nails, and tie a piece of ribbon to each end of the garland to conceal any exposed fishing line.

ROSEMARY
RECIPE 2:
FOCAL
ARRANGEMENT

————

INGREDIENTS

6 rosemary branches

6 stems of asclepias

4 stems of delphinium

5 pears

MATERIALS

Medium vase

3 wooden skewers

**A couple of pears placed next to this fragrant arrangement give the impression that they've just fallen from the branch.**

1.  Trim and add three branches of rosemary to the left side of the vase, and three branches to the right side.

2.  Trim and add four stems of asclepias to the front center of the arrangement, and two longer stems to the left side.

3.  Trim and add the stems of delphinium at the back to create the highest point of the arrangement.

4.  Skewer three pears and add to the front right side of the arrangement so that they rest on the edge of the vase, and place two pears on the surface just below the skewered pears.

## ROSEMARY
# RECIPE 3:
## WREATH

────────

### INGREDIENTS

6 large rosemary
branches

9 pears

### MATERIALS

Wire wreath frame

Medium-gauge wire

Embroidery needle

Start with the wire wreath
frame.

2 Attach three branches of rosemary to
the frame with medium-gauge wire—one
branch to the left and two to the right.
The stems should meet at the bottom of
the frame.

3 Attach another rosemary branch to the
right side of the frame, concealing the
stem by tucking it slightly under the
lower branch.

4 Use wire to attach another rosemary branch
to the left side of the frame, concealing its
stem with the lower branch's foliage. Wire
each pear individually (see page 16) and
attach them to the bottom of the wreath in
a cluster. Attach the final piece of rosemary
on the top left to fully conceal the frame.

Rosemary winds up the frame on either side of this wreath and meets in the center, evoking Olympian laurel crowns.

WINTER

*acacia*

*ivy*

*succulent*

# ACACIA

Acacia's fuzzy mini-pom-poms line the full branches of this tree and shrub, the most common varieties of which are from Australia. The bright yellow blooms stand out nicely against a palette of dark bush ivy berries, a few muted succulents, and dramatic amaryllis blooms. Word to the wise: Acacia blooms can give off a considerable amount of pollen, so beware if you have allergy-prone folks in your household.

*amaryllis*

*succulent*

*succulent*

ACACIA

# RECIPE 1:
## GARLAND

———

### INGREDIENTS

4 sprigs of acacia
branch

### MATERIALS

Twine

Medium-gauge wire

Four 6-inch pieces
of ribbon

**A group of acacia miniwreaths comes together quickly for a simple yet celebratory garland.**

1. Cut a piece of twine to the desired length of your garland.

2. Take one sprig of acacia and bend it into a loop. Attach the tip to the end with medium-gauge wire.

3. Repeat with the remaining three sprigs.

4. To finish, tie the loops onto the twine with the ribbon.

### INGREDIENTS

3 branches of acacia

3 branches of ivy

5 wired succulents
(see page 16)

### MATERIALS

Floral tape

1 yard of ribbon

**An unstructured swag on your door is just as welcoming as a wreath, and so easy to pull together.**

1. Gather the acacia and ivy and secure with floral tape.

2. Attach two wired succulents at the base of the swag, and the remaining three succulents toward the center.

3. Finish by wrapping the ribbon around the stems to conceal the tape and hang the swag.

## ACACIA
# RECIPE 3:
### WREATH

___

### INGREDIENTS

6 branches of ivy

6 branches of acacia

3 wired succulents
(see page 16)

3 wired amaryllis
blooms (see page 16)

### MATERIALS

Double-ring wreath
frame

Paddle wire

Attach two ivy branches to
the upper left of the double-
ring wreath frame with
paddle wire.

2 Wire two acacia branches to the frame
just below the ivy, and secure them with
paddle wire.

3 Continually wrapping with paddle wire,
alternate two ivy branches and two
acacia branches as you work your way
around the frame.

4 Attach the wired succulents to the
bottom of the frame using their wire
ends, and finish by attaching the wired
amaryllis blooms, two on the left side of
the succulents and one on the right side.

When you're ready to take down this wreath,
the succulents can be removed and planted.

*heather*

*hyacinth*

*anemone*

# CAMELLIA

If you're looking for a hardy, big-blooming flower to sweep away the winter blues, look no further than the camellia. Winter is when this little evergreen puts out some of its best buds, which give way to flowers thick with pink or white (or sometimes both) petals. Camellia blooms don't hold their petals long after being cut, but the leaves last a very long time. Hyacinth, heather, and anemone round out a colorful collection perfect for warmer winter days and just in time for Valentine's Day.

*camellia*

———

**INGREDIENTS**

6 camellia blooms

14 hyacinth blooms

3 sprigs of heather

2 anemones

**MATERIALS**

7 low bowls
of various sizes

**A simple, low collection of blooms is perfect for a coffee table, where the arrangement can best be observed from above.**

1. Place a collection of low bowls on a display surface and add a small amount of water to each bowl.

2. Add the assorted blooms to the bowls in a pleasing composition.

---

### INGREDIENTS

4 stems of hyacinth,
heads removed to
yield 65 blooms

1 camellia branch

### MATERIALS

Needle

Thread

1 yard of ribbon

**A chain of nested hyacinth blooms and a single pink ribbon transform a camellia branch into a fanciful swag.**

1. Using a needle and thread, thread through twenty-five hyacinth blooms on one piece of thread, and forty hyacinth blooms on a second piece of thread. Attach the ends of both pieces of thread to each end of a camellia branch.

2. Finish by tying the ribbon to the stem end of the branch and hang.

### INGREDIENTS

4 stems of heather

1 camellia branch

5 anemones

### MATERIALS

Wire wreath frame

Medium-gauge wire

1 Start with the wire wreath frame.

2 Take one long stem of heather and place it along the left half of the frame, securing it with medium-gauge wire so that the stem curves around the frame.

3 Take another stem of heather and attach it to the right half of the frame with wire.

4 Place the camellia branch across the frame diagonally and secure it with wire. Finish by tucking in the anemones at the lower center and right side of the frame. Trim and tuck in two short stems of heather to balance the composition.

The anemones in this simple wreath will last only a short while, so plan on a one-night event. The camellia and heather will dry nicely.

*red dogwood*

*leucadendron*

# CEDAR

Cedar is a temperate-weather evergreen with a flexible personality: it's as comfortable perched above a California beach as it is hanging on your mantel. A few of our favorite winter reds alongside some fragrant fans of cedar create a somewhat modern, muted version of the traditional Christmas colors. All the ingredients dry well and add uncommon shape and texture to the collection.

*cedar*

*Christmas bush*

*pepperberry*

# RECIPE 1:
## GARLAND

---

### INGREDIENTS

26 sprigs of cedar branches

48 sprigs of pepperberry

### MATERIALS

Bind wire

Paddle wire

**Cedar and pepperberry work together to form a trio of delicate garlands.**

1. Cut three pieces of bind wire to the desired lengths of your garlands. Divide the ingredients into three piles of a similar size: one with cedar, one with pepperberry, one with cedar and pepperberry.

2. Lay a sprig of cedar on a piece of bind wire and wrap with paddle wire to attach it. Continue attaching single sprigs of cedar as you work your way down the garland.

3. Use the same method to make the second garland from pepperberry sprigs.

4. Complete the last garland using the same method, this time alternating sprigs of cedar and pepperberry.

CEDAR
# RECIPE 2:
## WREATH

---

### INGREDIENTS

15 cedar branches

2 branches of
dogwood

3 branches of
leucadendron

4 stems of
Christmas bush

12 sprigs of
pepperberry

### MATERIALS

Double-ring
wreath frame

Paddle wire

**A flourished tail saves this wreath from holiday mundanity.**

1.  Attach the cedar branches to the double-ring wreath frame using paddle wire, making sure to cover the stem of the previous branch as you go. Attach the longest piece of cedar so that it cascades from the bottom of the frame toward the left.

2.  Tuck in the branches of dogwood at the bottom left, and tuck in the leuacadendron branches in a cluster on the right.

3.  Tuck in the stems of Christmas bush on the upper-left side of the wreath. Finish by adding clusters of pepperberry throughout.

# RECIPE 3:
## WALL HANGING

___

### INGREDIENTS

10 dogwood branches

6 leucadendron
branches

6 stems of
Christmas bush

7 cedar branches

5 sprigs of
pepperberry

### MATERIALS

Medium-gauge wire

1 Lay down seven dogwood branches vertically parallel to one another. Weave another branch through horizontally and attach it with medium-gauge wire on both ends.

2 Weave the remaining two dogwood branches horizontally across the middle and top of the wall hanging. Attach the branches with wire on both ends.

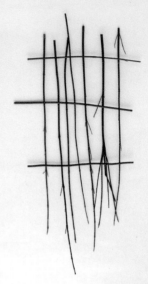

3 Weave five branches of leucadendron through the dogwood frame, skipping over some of the branches as necessary depending on the flexibility of the leucadendron.

4 Weave two stems of Christmas bush and five cedar branches throughout the dogwood frame. Tuck in the remaining branch of leucadendron, four stems of Christmas bush, and two cedar branches throughout. Finish by tucking in the sprigs of pepperberry in clusters across the piece.

These ingredients would work well in a wreath or
traditional arrangement, but a little imagination
turns them into a botanical tapestry.

*ilex*

*redwood*

# ILEX

When the ilex bush loses its leaves, branches filled with dense clusters of red berries are revealed, a welcome sight as the first frost begins to set in. Ilex holds its fruit a ways into winter, providing the woodland birds a nice light snack (they are toxic for humans and some animals). Since ilex (also known as winterberry) can sometimes be devoid of foliage, add a fan of redwood and some holly leaves around this merry bunch. Holly branches have a bite, so be mindful when handling them.

*holly*

ILEX
# RECIPE 1:
## CENTERPIECE

———

### INGREDIENTS
2 holly sprigs

2 redwood sprigs

2 ilex branches

### MATERIALS
5 log slices

**A variety of log slices holds a little forest of sprigs perfect for lining the length of a holiday dining table.**

1. Drill stem-sized holes into log slices.

2. Trim the ingredients to varying heights and place in the drilled holes in a pleasing arrangement.

ILEX
# RECIPE 2:
## WALL HANGING

———

### INGREDIENTS

1 redwood branch
with cones

1 holly branch

1 ilex branch

### MATERIALS

2 yards of ribbon
cut into 3 pieces

Branch

Floral glue

**A panel of seasonal ingredients is a great wreath alternative to herald in the holidays.**

1. Use floral glue to attach various bits and pieces of redwood, holly, and ilex branches to the three pieces of ribbon in a pleasing arrangement.

2. When the glue has dried, wrap the tops of the ribbons around the branch and secure them with floral glue. Wait until all the glue has dried before hanging.

Start with a loosely woven honeysuckle wreath frame.

2 Tuck in three ilex branches on the top left side of the frame.

3 Place the redwood branches facing in opposite directions on the bottom of the wreath and wire in place. Tuck the remaining ilex branch into the bottom of the wreath on the right side.

4 Tuck the holly branches into the bottom of the wreath so that they arc out in different directions.

A few basic branches come together in a snap to make a seasonal statement wreath.

# JUNIPER

There are many different kinds of juniper, but they usually share the same characteristics: scale-like leaves, blue-gray berries, and a strong fragrance that smells like either pine or gin (a drink derived from the plant). This evergreen's unique branches inspire a collection that's almost aquatic in nature.

*various branches*

*cymbidium orchid*

*air plant*

*winterbud (sweet huck)*

*juniper*

*air plant*

JUNIPER
# RECIPE 1:
## PLACE SETTING

———

### INGREDIENTS
3 bare branches,
cut into 9 pieces
of similar lengths

### MATERIALS
Three 4-inch pieces
of ribbon

**Gather tiny bundles of "firewood" and bind with colorful ribbon to create fanciful place settings or gift toppers.**

1. Bundle the branch pieces in sets of three and tie with ribbon.

2. Cut V-shapes into ends of the ribbons.

# RECIPE 2:
## WALL HANGING

———

### INGREDIENTS
1 juniper branch

3 wired air plants

### MATERIALS
1 yard of ribbon

Thin-gauge wire

**Cradle a collection of air plants on a single juniper branch for a simple, impactful display.**

1. Attach a piece of ribbon to each end of the juniper branch for hanging.

2. Wire the air plants onto the branch next to the ribbon and hang on the wall.

# JUNIPER
# RECIPE 3:
## CENTERPIECE

———

### INGREDIENTS

2 juniper branches

2 wired cymbidium
orchid blooms

3 wired air plants

### MATERIALS

1 bare branch

Medium-gauge wire

**A long bare branch becomes a catchall for a drift of orchids and air plants.**

1. Lay the branch across your display surface. On the right side,
   attach the juniper branches facing in opposite directions and
   wire them in place.

2. Attach the cymbidium orchids in the middle of the juniper
   branches.

3. Finish by attaching the air plants to surround the orchids.

## JUNIPER
# RECIPE 4:
### WREATH

––––––––

### INGREDIENTS

8 heavy bare branches

8 juniper branches

5 winter bud branches

9 wired cymbidium
orchid blooms

7 wired air plants

### MATERIALS

Grapevine wreath
frame

Medium-gauge wire

1 Lay two bare branches across the top of the grapevine wreath frame and secure them with medium-gauge wire.

2 Continue adding bare branches around the wreath, securing with wire as you go.

3 Tuck in six juniper branches around the wreath.

4 Tuck in the winterbud branches around the wreath. Attach clusters of cymbidium orchids around the wreath. Finish by attaching the air plants around the orchids, and tucking in the remaining two juniper branches.

An ethereal crown of branches comes together
to make a wild-reaching wreath.

# PINE

Although pine is synonymous with Christmas and all its trappings, it's easier than you think to change your impression of it. On paper, pairing pine with ranunculus, eucalyptus, minicarnations, and kumquats may seem a bit out there, but this disparate group manages to find harmony. In addition to the heavenly pine-menthol-citrus fragrance that follows it, festive colors come together to create a cheerful and fun grouping.

*eucalyptus*

*ranunculus*

*minicarnation*

*pine*

*kumquat*

# RECIPE 1:
## PLACE SETTING

———

### INGREDIENTS
1 sprig of pine

2 sprigs of eucalyptus

1 sprig of kumquat

### MATERIALS
Floral tape

12-inch piece of ribbon

**A small posy packs a punch of fragrance when pine, eucalyptus, and kumquat are the players.**

1. Gather the ingredients and secure with floral tape just below the blooms.

2. Tie the ribbon so that it conceals the floral tape and trim the stems 1 inch below where the ribbon is tied.

# RECIPE 2:
## WREATH

---

### INGREDIENTS

6 pine branches

5 branches of kumquat

10 branches of eucalyptus

2 sprays of minicarnations

3 wired blooms of ranunculus

### MATERIALS

Wire wreath frame

Paddle wire

**These ingredients work together to create an unexpected palette and a festive wreath that's seasonal, but far from traditional.**

1. Gather a bundle using an assortment of pine, kumquat, and eucalyptus and attach it to the wire wreath frame with paddle wire.

2. Continue to make similar bundles alternating long and short ingredients, and add them to the frame so that each new bundle covers the stems of the previous one. Wrap continuously with paddle wire as you go until the frame is covered.

3. Finish by tucking the sprays of minicarnations into the bottom of the wreath and attaching the ranunculus blooms.

# PINE
# RECIPE 3:
## MOBILE

———

### INGREDIENTS

11 branches of
eucalyptus

7 ranunculus blooms

9 minicarnation blooms

5 sprigs of kumquat

6 kumquat fruits

1 sprig of pine

### MATERIALS

Wire frame

Medium-gauge wire

Embroidery needle

Fishing line

**1** Use medium-gauge wire to attach six branches of eucalyptus at equal distances apart around the wire frame. Gather the free ends of the eucalyptus above the frame and wire them together.

**2** Attach a branch of eucalyptus to the bottom of the frame at the same joining location as the branch above. Bend the piece across the frame to the opposite side. Repeat the process with two more branches of eucalyptus.

**3** Attach the remaining two branches of eucalyptus around the outside of the frame to conceal it. Hang in place with a long piece of fishing line.

**4** Alternating their order, attach five stems of ranunculus, minicarnations, and kumquat around the frame with wire. To make the tassel, thread the remaining two ranunculus, four minicarnations, and three kumquats onto the fishing line with the embroidery needle and attach to the bottom of the mobile. Finish by wiring three kumquats at the top and a pine sprig to the tassel.

Inspired by Polish *pajaki*, a traditional folk craft where paper is folded and tied into complex mobiles, this project uses flowers and branches to build a floral "chandelier."

# PUSSY WILLOW

With sleek shoots and silky flowers, pussy willow is a pared-down branch with few frills. Its delicate, fuzzy flowers, known as *catkins*, are their only adornment and perfectly punctuate its dark bark. Pussy willow's woody shoots hold up well over time and dry nicely and are complemented by bleached pinecones and blue-green spruce.

*pussy willow*

*bleached pinecones*

*spruce*

*bleached pinecones*

PUSSY WILLOW
## RECIPE 1:
PLACE SETTING

————

**INGREDIENTS**

3 small bleached
pinecones

**MATERIALS**

Three 12-inch pieces
of ribbon

**Bleached pinecones can be purchased at craft stores, but regular pinecones
work just as well for this simple project.**

1. Tie a ribbon around the top of each pinecone for hanging.

PUSSY WILLOW
# RECIPE 2:
## MOBILE

---

### INGREDIENTS
6 bleached pinecones

1 spruce branch

### MATERIALS
Twine

Fishing line

**Pinecones hang like snowflakes below a branch of blue spruce in this simple mobile.**

1. Cut six pieces of twine and tie one to each pinecone.

2. Tie a piece of fishing line to both ends of the spruce branch and hang.

3. Tie the ends of the twine along the branch so the cones hang at varying heights.

# RECIPE 3:
## WALL HANGING

---

### INGREDIENTS

9 pussy willow
branches

### MATERIALS

String

Glue

Three 1-yard
pieces of ribbon

**A wintery web-like wall hanging is the perfect project to show off pussy willow's long, lean personality.**

1. Lay the pussy willow branches across one another to form a circular shape, then lash them together at the center with string.

2. Glue one end of a piece of ribbon to the center of the web. Once it is secure, weave the ribbon around the center of the circle, running it over and under each branch and winding toward the outside of the circle. When you finish weaving the ribbon, glue the end to a branch to secure it.

3. Continue to weave and secure in the same manner with the remaining ribbons, gluing the end of each ribbon. Use the lashed center as the support when hanging.

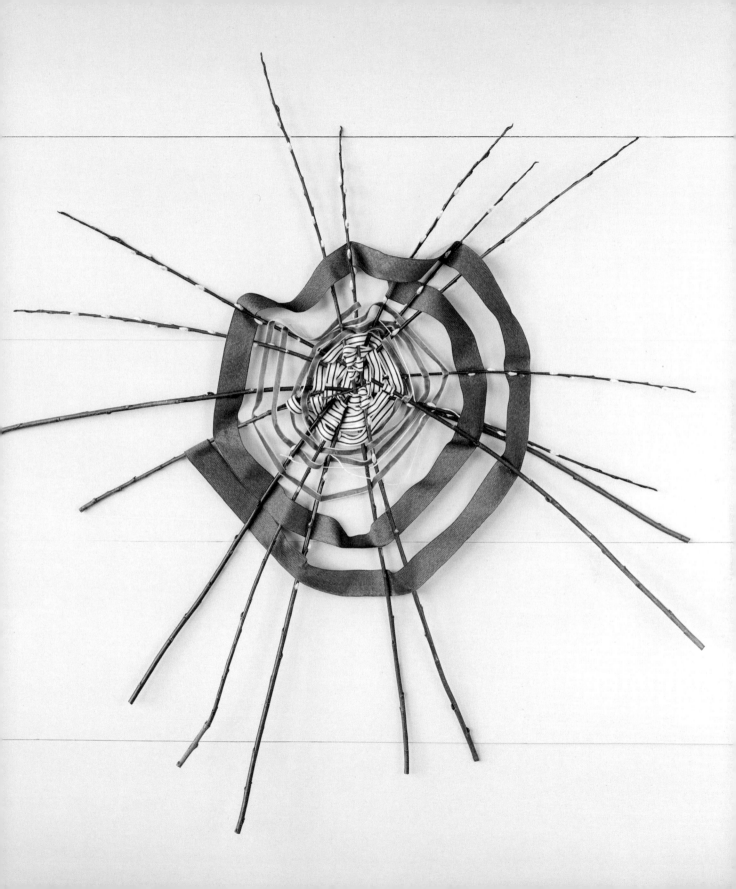

## PUSSY WILLOW
# RECIPE 4:
### WREATH

———

### INGREDIENTS

4 spruce branches

5 pussy willow
branches

10 bleached and
wired pinecones

### MATERIALS

Grapevine wreath
frame

Medium-gauge wire

1 | Start with the grapevine
wreath frame.

2 | Bend three spruce branches around
the frame and secure them with wire.
Allow the branches to hang over the
wreath as desired.

3 | Bend the pussy willow branches around
the wreath, tucking in the ends to secure.

4 | Attach the pinecones around the wreath
at pleasing locations. Finish by tucking
in the last spruce branch on the upper
left side.

Cool winter colors and textures come together
to create a simple seasonal wreath.

# TALLOW

The long, winding fingers of the tallow tree are topped with sleek white berries that last throughout the winter and beyond. Its attractive little berries have been so popular with local fauna that the tallow tree has spread its seed far and wide and is now an invasive species in some parts of the United States. Pairing tallow with narcissus (commonly forced during winter months) and aromatic bay laurel hints at the spring brightness to come.

*narcissus*

*bay laurel*

*narcissus*

*tallow*

———

### INGREDIENTS

3 sprigs of bay laurel

20 stems of narcissus

3 sprigs of tallow

### MATERIALS

5 small vases

**A minicollection of wintry ingredients running down the center of a table highlights their solo and mixed appeal.**

1.  Gather five posies so that each ingredient has one vase to itself and the other two vases hold a combination of the ingredients.

2.  Trim and add one posy to each vase.

———

### INGREDIENTS

36 sprigs of bay laurel

24 sprigs of tallow

### MATERIALS

Twine

Paddle wire

Spanish moss

**Bind bay laurel onto a simple piece of twine to create a fresh, long-lasting garland.**

1.  Gather three bay laurel sprigs and two sprigs of tallow and attach the bundle to a length of twine with paddle wire.

2.  Continue to gather and attach bundles down the length of the twine, adding each new bundle over the stems of the previous one. Tuck pieces of Spanish moss between the bundles to finish.

## TALLOW RECIPE 3: WREATH

---

### INGREDIENTS

5 bay laurel branches

5 tallow branches

15 stems of narcissus

### MATERIALS

Wire wreath frame

Medium-gauge wire

Spanish moss

Spray snow

3 rubber bands

3 small plastic bags

3 paper towels

Start with the wire wreath frame.

2 Bend three bay laurel branches around the frame and attach each branch with medium-gauge to secure.

3 Nestle the tallow branches into the bay laurel branches around the wreath, securing them with the wire.

4 Bag five narcissus stems (see page 18) and attach to the right side of the wreath with wire. Bag two more narcissus bunches and attach one to the lower right side and one to the left. Attach the final bay laurel branches to the left side, concealing the bags with Spanish moss, and spray with spray snow as desired.

Clumps of narcissus appear to sprout from snowdrifts in this whimsical wreath.

*waxflower*

# WAXFLOWER

Similar to heather, waxflower has needle-like leaves, and its masses of pink and white flowers arrive in winter full force. Other winter bloomers like Asian magnolias put out magnificent pink buds that open into large, blooming saucers, while holiday-ready hypericum and pine mix and mingle appropriately to complement a colorful collection.

*pine*

*hypericum*

*magnolia*

WAXFLOWER
# RECIPE 1:
## FOCAL
## ARRANGEMENT

———

### INGREDIENTS

10 waxflower branches
of two different colors

### MATERIALS

Medium-sized vase

**Waxflower is usually used as a filler flower, but different varieties massed together make a bold two-toned arrangement.**

1. Trim and add five branches of one color waxflower to the left side of the vase, and five branches of another color to the right side.

### INGREDIENTS

10 waxflower branches

5 magnolia branches

5 pine sprigs

10 stems of hypericum

### MATERIALS

Double-ring wreath
frame

Paddle wire

**A seasonal wreath of pink and purple will be a welcome surprise to guests.**

1. Gather a bundle of the ingredients and attach to the double-ring wreath frame using paddle wire.

2. Continue to make and attach bundles in the same manner, varying the amount and length of ingredients as desired, until the entire frame is covered.

## WAXFLOWER
# RECIPE 3:
## SWAG

---

### INGREDIENTS

1 magnolia branch

9 sprigs of waxflower

9 stems of hypericum

### MATERIALS

Paddle wire

1 yard of ribbon

**1** Start with the magnolia branch.

**2** Gather a bundle of three sprigs of waxflower and three stems of hypericum and use paddle wire to attach it to the left side of the branch.

**3** Make a second bundle with the same ingredients and attach it so that it overlaps the stems of the first bundle, facing the same direction.

**4** Make a third bundle with the remaining ingredients and attach it to the branch in the opposite direction, concealing the stems under the other bundles. Finish by attaching a piece of ribbon to both ends of the branch and hang.

How much can one magnolia branch hold? A lot. Give it all you've got with this colorful swag consumed with waxflowers and hypericum berries.

## THANK YOU

To Lia T for being the best secret ghost, Matt for building the wall that made it all possible, Ron and Kathi for their never-ending love and support, Clydie for keeping us safe, Matteo for building everything and not complaining, Kay and Jon for passing down their love for nature's wilderness, Ever for letting her mom work so much, Katie for being so sweet and letting us boss her around all the time, Paige for her amazing talent at capturing natural light, Steve for being an awesome babysitter and friend, Miriam for being so willing to help, Lia R for letting our creativity run wild, Michelle for her beautiful design and Sibylle for letting us have our way sometimes, Kitty for always having our back, the bad-boy crew for being so bad, and to all our helpers who emptied endless trugs, swept the floor, and got us lunch—you know who you are.

## ABOUT THE AUTHORS

**ALETHEA HARAMPOLIS** and **JILL RIZZO** are the authors of Artisan's *The Flower Recipe Book*, praised by the *New York Times* as "a beautifully illustrated and practical guide to the ephemeral art of fresh-flower arranging." They run floral design company Studio Choo in San Francisco, where they create wild, sculptural arrangements and teach a variety of flower-arranging classes. Their work has been featured in the *New York Times*, *Real Simple*, *Redbook*, *Country Living*, and *Brides* and on Design*Sponge, Apartment Therapy, Kinfolk, and Remodelista.